For Mum and Dad
– thanks for everything

SENATE BOOKS

Published by Senate Books, 2006
Norfolk Court, 1 Norfolk Road, Rickmansworth, Herts WD3 1LA

Text copyright 2005 Richard Fox
Main photography John Eckart and Chris Leah
Additional food styling Gordon Gellatly
Sub-editor Adam Gray
Design concept Andy Goodman
Design layout Darren Westlake

ISBN 1-901268-16-0
Printed in Thailand

Contents

YOU CAN'T BE A REAL
COUNTRY UNLESS
YOU HAVE A BEER
AND AN AIRLINE.
IT HELPS IF YOU
HAVE SOME KIND
OF A FOOTBALL
TEAM, OR SOME
NUCLEAR WEAPONS,
BUT AT THE VERY
LEAST YOU
NEED A BEER.
FRANK ZAPPA

Post-party breakfast

S&SARNIES **30**

NTURE **78**

24

CONTENTS

Let me introduce you...

The last 20 years of my life have been spent professionally pursuing the art of taste and flavour; service, environment, cooking and atmosphere. It's pure hedonism really, but somehow I've managed to carve out a living for myself – albeit a miniscule one at times. It has to be said that as soon as you start down that road of sensory pleasure for a living, you stop being in control of your own life – your life pursuits control you, and you either fight it – and subject yourself to a life of stress and anguish, or you roll with it – and see what pleasures avail themselves to you. Sometimes it's all got a bit out of hand and the boundaries of good taste have somehow got merged with those of bad taste. But as my mate Andy has always reminded me: 'if you live life on the edge, you get a better view'.

That is precisely how it is, and what an adventure it's been. It's taken me from the 'brown cafés' of old Amsterdam to the beat of New Orleans where great food, music and booze meld together under one buzzing roof. It's not been pretty at times: I've busted my ass in the sweaty kitchens of London, opened bars for bohemians in the provinces and 'maître d' in the ostentatious environments of 1980's 'hoteldom'. But one thing has remained constant throughout this journey – my pursuit of taste and flavour in their myriad forms.

BBQ entertainment Cuban style

Over time, I've found increasingly that this mainly comes through simplicity, where the secret of the meal experience is more in the hands of the ingredients than the person cooking. And I'm not on my own here: In the last few years we've seen an exponential growth in Farmers' markets; regional, seasonal classics are back on menus, and while ethnic cuisine has become ingrained in our own food culture, sourcing produce has become provenance led. Wherever there's a taste experience to be had based on artisan methods of rearing and production, there's a story to tell with it and believe me, that story translates directly to the experience when sampled from the plate.

So, how come we've been quaffing wine at break-neck speed for the last fifteen years? After all, Northern Europe – and indeed the countries where our ethnic cuisine originates are steeped in the grain not the grape. Don't get me wrong, I love a fine wine as much as anyone, it's just a case of getting a sense of balance – and, of course, discovering new and exciting flavours, which, although having been around for centuries, if not thousands of years, have, until recently, been lost amongst the bland, one-dimensional beers that have been mass-produced to satisfy the thirst of a session-drinking culture. This has given beer in this country a bad name.

Comradeship!

It's a Learning experience

Cooking with friends

In fact, beer has been enjoyed as a beverage of gastronomic importance since the beginning of time – well, certainly as far back as the ancient Egyptians, who revered it so much they got buried with grains of barley and pitchers to sustain them in the after-life. Moving forward in time, King Wenceslas – living up to his good name – imposed the death penalty for anyone caught exporting his prized Saaz hops, which are still used to make the finer Pilsner lagers. In medieval England it was a floggable offence to serve poor quality beer. The point is: you don't generate this kind of hoohah about just any beverage. This kind of passion, excitement and appreciation only comes when there's something really worth shouting about. The stylish cities of northern Europe – Prague, Amsterdam, Berlin, Brussels and London have their traditions firmly steeped in the grain rather than the grape, and, once you scratch below the surface of the more populist brands, we uncover a range of artisan beers to rival the finest châteaux. From floral, honeyed and buttery Pilsner Urquell to light and zesty Paulaner Hefe-weiss bier, these are beverages with serious gastronomic credentials. Of course several thousand years is a long time to perfect any recipe, but it's only very recently that we have, once again, begun to appreciate their style, balance, and complexity.

In this book, beer is no more of a gimmick than the artisan produce I urge you to use with it. Beer is in fact, a metaphor for provenance and flavour. The beers represented in this book have a tradition of craftsmanship. These beers are world-class recipes in their own right. It would be a shame then to combine those centuries of flavour-driven refinement with some intensively reared, chemically-fed and inhumanely killed piece of bland, tasteless meat, fish or vegetable. Most of these recipes will work perfectly well if the beer is omitted – other liquid ingredients could easily be substituted. Having said that, the inclusion of the beer undoubtedly gives an extra dimension to the dish – think of it as a secret weapon in your arsenal of seasonings. Also, by including beer in the recipe, it's a great excuse to analyse the flavours and see what a fabulous accompaniment to food beer really is. And then of course there's the human element which is as important to the meal experience as the food itself – the beers become a talking point around the table, a point of difference; there's a story to tell, a history which manifests itself as flavour, and just plain and simple good times brought on by flavour-fuelled, good old-fashioned booze. Tip, tipple, experiment, and above all enjoy a new and incredible journey of taste and flavour. **Cheers.**

It's all about PASSION!

Beer styles

Belgian classics

I believe it is customary to talk about the brewing process at this point, but quite frankly it would probably bore you into oblivion – and there's plenty of information in other books and on the web if you really want to know. Let's face it – you don't need to know about malolactic fermentation to appreciate a fine red Burgundy. But, just for the record: take a load of barley (and sometimes wheat), germinate it, turn it into malt and then mix it with hot water; drain off the water, add a sackful of hops and then ferment it by adding yeast. Then it matures – unlike what happens to us when we consume too much of it. Okay, that all sounds a little flippant – I'm just saying we don't need to get into the science to enjoy the experience. It should be said, however, that brewing really is an art. Recipes can be centuries old, and the brewer should be as revered as the crafted brews he produces.

So, without getting into a chemistry lesson, it's worth noting what lager is, and how it differs from other beer categories. The word lager is derived from the German word "lagern" meaning 'to store'. It uses bottom-fermenting yeasts – as oppose to top-fermenting yeasts found in real ales, bottle-conditioned beers and more artisan brews.

In a nutshell, bottom-fermenting yeasts tend to be more stable and predictable, but don't give the depth of flavour and complexity found in beers made from top-fermenting yeasts. Now we've got that over with, just one more word about wild yeasts – mainly found in the lambic fruit beers of Belgium, and worth mentioning just because they're so damn good, and feature pretty heavily in this book. Basically, rather than scientific chemist-types adding carefully controlled yeast strains to closed vessels, wild yeasts float down onto the exposed surface of the beer through open windows and slats in the roof, in a rather random fashion. The results are magnificent. Enough said. The variations within each of those processes, the proportion of ingredients themselves, and other natural flavourings are as infinite as the different flavours generated.

Sadly, in this country there is a tendency to look at beer as a rather one-dimensional product in terms of appearance, flavour and texture – it always seems to be wine that achieves the moral high ground here. But, to think of beer purely in terms of bitter or lager is like perceiving fish as only cod or haddock. Nothing wrong with either of these – except look at what you'd be missing out on by dismissing salmon, fresh tiger prawns, lobster, oysters, red-snapper, sea bass – I could go on.

A summary of beer types, and examples

Lager Generally, a clean refreshing beer, which, at the lower end, can be bland, and lacking real taste. Pilsners fall into the lager category, the best of which are honeyed, floral, buttery, and can be considered world-class brews. Classic Pilsner lagers are Pilsner Urquell and Budweiser Budvar (not to be confused with the American Budweiser).

Ales A very broad term meaning top-fermented beers. Too many varieties to put under one heading, but most commonly brewed in the UK. Hoppy, fruity and complex. Within this classification, however, colour and flavour variations are manifold. For our purposes simply bitter, India Pale Ale, strong, and old ales.

Bitter A classic, standard ale, with a well-hopped bitterness. The finest have good character and aroma, are well balanced and floral. There are hundreds...

IPA Originally brewed to satisfy the thirst of the British in the colonies and therefore highly hopped to preserve it on those long sea journeys. Check out Deuchars IPA and Marstons Old Empire.

Strong and old ales Rich, dark and fruity! Many exciting flavours typify these beers, from prunes and sultanas, to apples and pears. Try Fullers 1845 or Greene King's Strong Suffolk Ale.

Wheat beer Normally Belgian or German. Today more widespread. Using wheat as well as Barley; often cloudy with sediment adding to character and flavour. Refreshing, citrussy, and herbal, with minimal bitterness. Hoegaarden (Belgium), Paulaner (Germany) and O'Hanlon's (UK) are fine examples.

Fruit Beer A personal favourite, and an invaluable tool to convert the non-believer. Not alcopops, but world-class artisan brews. Most commonly from the lambic-producing region of Belgium, they utilise real fruit, often macerated over many months in oak barrels. The best are a perfect balance of sweet and sour, with a light Champagne-like effervescence. Check out Liefmans Framboise (raspberry), or Belle Vue Kriek (cherry).

Porter and Stout Porter was the forerunner of stout, but both are similar in character – dark and creamy with notes of chocolate and a full roasted bitterness; however, Stout is generally stronger and darker than porter – and lingeringly dry. Guiness is by far the most famous example, however Fullers London Porter is a classic.

Trappist beer Only six breweries – 5 Belgian, 1 Dutch. Brewed by Trappist Monks, these beers are regarded as some of the world's finest. Incredibly complex, and, at times, astonishingly alcoholic (14% abv). Bottle-conditioned varieties can be aged like fine wines. Chimay and Westmalle are widely known.

Abbaye beer Effectively copies of Trappist beers – but fine, nonetheless. Very much in the Trappist style, but because they are commercially-brewed , they lack the name. Leffe is a particularly fine example.

Bière de Garde From the beer-producing region of northern France, these beers have the same artisan qualities as France's fine wines. They tend to be strong with great balance and complexity and are often in corked bottles secured with a wire cage.

Barley wine Not wine at all, but very strong beer – up to 13 or 14%. The best varieties, such as Thomas Hardy Ale, have rich, dark fruit complexity, and have a certain brandy quality in their taste.

It should noted that there are many other styles such as smoked and Bock beers (mostly German), Saison beers – in Champagne-like bottles and Vienna style beers. These are magnificent and are great fun to source from independent, specialized retailers who will be delighted to share their knowledge with you, and make suggestions on how they will match with food.

Tasting

If you're going to get into some serious beer 'cheffery', or, if you just want to start the exciting process of discovering new food and beer flavour matchings, you can enhance the whole experience by adopting some quality tasting procedures. Not only does this offer you the best chance of fully appreciating all the nuances of flavour, but it will help give you inspiration for new recipes – it is also a ritual pleasure in itself. Just a quick word of warning: only pour an inch or so of beer into a tasting glass, wine glass or beer branded glassware. If you're tasting several beers, you'll be too intoxicated by the time you've finished to remember what you initially tasted. And secondly, you'll spill the contents all over yourself when swilling it around the glass.

Step 1 Appearance There are nearly as many different colours and hues to beer as there are flavours. From cloudy wheat beers to Pilsners, as crystal clear as a mountain stream; from spritzy as Champagne to still as tap water. Colours go from impenetrable black to almost white, with every shade of red, orange, yellow and brown making up the spectrum in between. The best way to assess the colour and hue of the beer is to hold the glass in front of a sheet of white paper. The most important thing when judging appearance is to ask yourself: 'does it look appetizing?' It should have you 'champing at the bit' to give it a swirl and inhale those heady aromas – which brings us nicely to the 'nose'.

Step 2 The nose Give the beer a good swill round in the glass – you'll see the wisdom of not over pouring here. This releases the aromas for you to inhale deeply. Don't be shy here – get those nostrils right in and prepare to reap the rewards. A good beer will have complexity and it will be harder therefore to pick out single scents. Things will come to you in fleeting moments only to be replaced by something else a second later. Concentrate hard and note down immediate gut feelings – however bizarre they may seem. You'll be surprised how many times your responses match the 'experts'. While I'm not suggesting you go through all this in your local boozer with your regular pint, you can see how much extra value and pleasure there is to be had from a single beer – and you haven't even tasted it yet!

Step 3 Taste and flavour Take a sip – breathing air over it as you do. Give it a little swirl around in your mouth (you experience different taste sensations on different parts of the tongue) i.e. sweet, sour, salty, bitter – and the new one: umami (ask the Japanese!). Flavour is experienced in the olfactory bulb at the back of the nose. Because of this, try and breathe out through your nose as you swallow for maximum flavour experience. Once again, a complex, well-balanced beer will offer different tastes and flavours over a time period. It could be hops and malt at the front,

caramel in the middle and a lingering fruit flavour on the finish. As with the nose, the sensations can be fleeting, so keep those instincts sharp.

Finally Eating and drinking is all about sensory pleasure, not theory and science. Any opportunity to further these great pleasures of life should be grasped with both hands. The world of good beer is vast – and still largely unexplored by most of us. So, whether you just a get a little more pleasure from your regular pint, or embark on a life-time's journey of flavour discovery, there's something life-enhancing about embracing the new world of beer.

CHEERS SALUTE SALUD PROST SANTÉ NA ZDRAVI AND ALL THE OTHERS THE WORLD OVER!

Beer & food matching

The fact that beer is used in all these recipes is just part of what this whole book is about – and only a tiny part of what beer's about per se. Obviously, if a particular beverage is used in a recipe, it's a good rule of thumb to suppose that the same drink may accompany the dish. What then, when we go out to eat and beer isn't used in the cooking process (which is going to be most of the time), – how do you know which beer – if beer at all? Hopefully, by absorbing bits of information in this book, there may be subliminal help at hand. If it only makes us question in a little more detail the flavours we experience, we can really start rollin' with our instincts – you'd be amazed how many times they work (in all aspects of life).

A short history lesson

"Te-henquet" Beer and food have been inextricably linked since the invention of beer by ancient civilisations thousands of years ago. The Pharaoh kings were so enamoured by their beer and food combos that they got buried with pitchers for beer and grain for bread to sustain them in the after-life. In fact, beer as a food accompaniment was held in such high esteem that 'bread and beer' was an Egyptian blessing, uttered something like: "Te-Henquet"

Obviously, if bread – and the kebab, were the only foods that could be linked with beer, we'd be on pretty fragile ground trying to make claims about its gastronomic significance. Fortunately history once again comes to the rescue. The Tudors and Elizabethans led the way with huge celebratory banquets with ales specially made to commemorate and accompany the events.

But to really understand the close relationship between food and beer, we need a bit of a geography lesson.

A short geography lesson

Any gourmet traveller will support the view that a nation's or climatic region's cuisine will have a beverage that has grown up alongside it – embracing the same customs, rituals, history, and raw materials as the food. For these reasons, it will generally be an appropriate beverage to accompany the food. It's strange, then, that we've been quaffing wine for the last twenty years at an alarmingly disproportionate rate to its suitability for the food it's accompanying. For a start, the vine growing areas of the world which yield decent wine are limited to two bands between 30 degrees and 50 degrees north and south of the Equator. This includes Southern Europe, Australia, South Africa, and parts of Argentina and Chile. That leaves the whole of South East Asia, most of south and central America and huge swathes of northern Europe including the Benelux countries, Scandinavia and of course, The UK. All these countries are renowned for producing craft beers of the highest quality. Beer is much better suited to the intensely spiced foods of India and South east Asia; the cured fish dishes of Scandinavia, the hearty stews of Belgium, and the rich game, sweet pork, casseroles and other regional British dishes that, thankfully, are making a return to our tables. Add to this the fact that ethnic cuisines have become ingrained in our own food culture, and the argument for beer is looking very strong indeed.

Why does it work? Whichever food and drink combination you go for, the drink should perform one, or a combination, of the following roles. It's these processes that bring out the best in the food, and in the drink. Subtle flavours, that on their own may not be apparent, suddenly jump out at you giving the whole experience a new flavour-fuelled dimension.

Complement On a broad basis, it could be said that a light, fresh beer will go with a light, fresh food such as fish;

Making mayo...

while a strong, darker beer will go better with a full-flavoured robust dish such as stew, casserole, game or red meat. Regard these principles as vague rules of thumb, and by no means the only way. On a more micro level, the fruitiness of a specific beer, such as the raspberry flavour of a lambic Framboise may perfectly accompany the fruit element of a dessert.

Contrast Contrasting is all about the principal of 'opposites attract' – and I'm sure we've all had experience of that phenomenon. A chocolate dessert is a fine example: the sweetness of the dessert contrasts with the inherent bitterness in ale. However, at the same time, there is comparing element, whereby that bitterness from the cocoa in good quality chocolate will match up with that same element in the beer. The most famous example of the contrast concept is Guinness and Oysters: the light, delicate, sweet flavoured oyster contrasts directly with the dark, roasted qualities in the beer – but it doesn't half work a treat!

Cut or Cleanse Beer will cut through spicy, fatty and rich food like a knife through butter. The palate is cleansed after each mouthful by the beer, and the lucky recipient is just left gagging for more. South East Asia provides some fine lager beers such as Singah from Thailand. Its dryness helps cut through the spiciness and the creaminess of Thai food, while the citrus notes continue to refresh the palate after each mouthful of food.

Regional Classics

While this is fine as a quick reference, easy-fix guide to food matching by beer type, it should never override personal preferences or new, left-field discoveries. **Nonetheless, it's a decent starting point for your own** journey of discovery.

Pilsner Being light, fruity, slightly honeyed with a dry finish, it will go with pretty much anything. Given its cutting and cleansing abilities however, it is perfect with fish and chips – a true gourmet meal when cooked with firm, fresh, fish in a light, crisp beer batter and a pile of home-made chips. It's equally at home with a slab of steak and a rich béarnaise sauce, or a fillet of oily fish such as salmon or mackerel. Its credentials alongside hot and spicy food are second to none.

Wheat beer A good wheat beer such as Belgian Hoegaarden or German Paulaner comes into its own with lightly poached salmon, or a firm white fish such as Swordfish or Kingfish. South East Asian dishes – rich in coriander and lemon grass – are perfect marriages.

Ales Match up British regional ales with regional or national classics: Sunday roast with a good malty, toffee-ish ale such as Morlands Old Speckled Hen; local, butcher-made sausages with the local brewery's flagship brew; grouse with the fabulous Scottish Fraoch (pronounced 'Frew-och'), made from heather, and just about any good ale with all manner

of cheese dishes, cured hams, and full-flavoured stews.

Trappist/Abbaye Beers Big, complex and intensely rich, these beers should be matched with similar foods: game, slow-roast pork and full-flavoured sausages are ideal. But they also make great dessert beers – for rich chocolate dishes, as well as steamed puddings, or sticky toffee pudding.

Fruit Beers Perhaps, gastronomically, these are the most versatile of beers. They're as at home with pâtés and parfaits of foie gras and chicken livers (and so much cheaper than a Sauternes), as they are with delicate fruit tarts. They are also a perfect match for fresh summer salads, and a great match for piquant salad dressings.

Porters and Stouts Contrast these dark, chocolatey, roasted brews with shell-fish such as oysters and lobster, or serve in port glasses to match up with a rich, bitter chocolate dessert. Quite astounding with Christmas pudding when flavours, previously left undetected, leap out at you quite unexpectedly.

BY EMBRACING BEER **AS A DRINK** WITH AS MUCH TO OFFER THE DINING EXPERIENCE AS WINE, WE START TO OPEN UP THIS WHOLE NEW WORLD OF FLAVOUR OPTIONS. AS CONSUMERS OF **GASTRONOMIC PLEASURES,** IT WOULD BE SELF-DEPRIVATION IN THE EXTREME NOT TO, AT THE VERY LEAST, **CONSIDER BEER** TO BE A VIABLE ALTERNATIVE TO ANY OTHER FOOD-FRIENDLY BEVERAGE.

Cooking with beer

"It's more than steak and ale pie"

It is often, and incorrectly, assumed that the only place beer has in the kitchen is in the chef's hand at the end of a hard night's service! While this tradition should be upheld at all costs, it's only one of the many roles beer can perform in the kitchen. When we think of cooking with alcoholic beverages, we tend to think firstly of wine, and then sherry, brandy, port, marsala, Noilly Prat – and if beer does get a look-in, then it's a token slug in a steak pie. Within the beer category, there is a greater wealth of texture, taste and flavour than across all the above kitchen-friendly beverages, thereby making it one of the most versatile of all cooking condiments.

Get stuck in my son!

"History strikes again"

The great nineteenth-century Epicurean, Escoffier, coined the term 'à la bière' to describe a dish cooked with beer. Before that, the Elizabethans used beer to casserole lamb with prunes and raisins. Beer batter was being prepared as far back as Tudor times. A celebrated Belgian chef, Raoul Morleghem, who cooked for heads of state in the 1950's, produced a definitive book of 300 recipes utilising beer in the cooking. Even in wine's spiritual home, a group of French gastronomes founded 'The Order of The Chope d'Or' (golden tankard) to further the 'gastronomic appreciation of beer'. What I'm saying is; beer is no 'flash-in-the-pan' culinary gimmick.

Beer is as diverse and adaptable an ingredient as the ubiquitous chicken's egg. Think of a cooking method and there's a type of beer that can be incorporated into it – slow roast, braise, poach, steam or sauté. Think salad dressings, marinades, chocolate desserts; parfaits and pâtés, even sushi and Szechwan. For all these and more, there's a brew that will give a lift here and a twist there. And the good news is there's nothing complicated

Poaching pears

Market day - Havana

about it. Just combine the smallest amount of common sense with an adventurous spirit and you're away.

Before we get into specifics, let's dispel a few myths about cooking with alcohol. Firstly, the quality of a finished dish is a reflection of the quality of ingredients used. So, the concept of using only cheap booze for cooking is fundamentally flawed. A quick jaunt to one of European neighbours in Brussels or Prague tells a very interesting story – the finest restaurants will have beer lists incorporating a huge variety of tastes, flavours and textures to satisfy every palate – and you can be assured that the kitchen will have a fine selection alongside the olive oil, sea salt, peppercorns and fresh herbs.

A few simple pointers

Use good quality beer Apply the same guidelines to cooking with beer as matching with food – remember: 'cut, contrast, cut and cleanse.' Be careful when 'reducing' beer i.e. boiling it until it reduces in volume to a specified level. It concentrates the bitterness. Consider therefore when to add the beer. If heavy reduction of a sauce is involved – wait to the end to add the beer. Or, use a beer very low in bitterness such as a wheat beer or lambic fruit beer. For long, slow cooking, beer can be added at the beginning of the process.

Beer in cooking, by method This shows the variety of cooking methods that lend themselves to 'cuisine à la bière'. The variations that can be achieved within each category are endless. Your imagination and time for experimentation are the only limiting factors.

Marinating For red meat, white meat and fish. A strong, darker beer is perfect for rich red meats. Beer is also – allegedly – high in tenderising enzymes, making it ideal for this 'cooking' method. For fish, a zesty, herb infused wheat beer such as Hoegaarden is perfect. Marinating liquids can also often be used in a cooking stock.

Ginger - an ancient beer ingredient

Cooking with beer

Biére à la cuisine – cooking in Paris

Braise/Casserole/Slow roast Full flavoured, strong beers such as a Belgian Trapppist, or Abbaye beer are perfect – as are the fabulous range of quality English bottled beers such as Fullers ESB, or Black Sheep Ale. These beers' fruitiness gives an extra depth of flavour to the finished dish.

Baking Try experimenting with different beers in bread dough. Just substitute a small amount of beer for water. For best results use a bottle-conditioned beer. These beers contain living yeast sediment. As far as cakes are concerned, try a little light beer in a sponge, or a chocolatey porter in a fruitcake.

Deep Frying Beer makes fabulous batter. From richly- flavoured batters for firm, white fish to a light Tempura batter for shellfish or vegetables. A slug of Yorkshire ale in a Yorkshire pudding batter should be de rigueur.

Salad Dressings This is one of the easiest and most rewarding ways to use beer in food. The lambic fruit beers are ideal with their high acidity, never mind their fabulous fruitiness.

Poaching Beer is an ideal poaching liquor for savoury or sweet, adding much more than just water. Figs and pears are good candidates, while fish or chicken can be poached in a fragrant wheat beer with added coriander, lemon or lime juice.

Steaming Steaming mussels in beer was a 'eureka' moment in my early days of cooking with beer – but it's the only way! So why not use it as a steaming medium for other fish dishes?

Sauces Wheat beer in a cream sauce, a pan de-glazed with a fruit beer before adding a rich game jus, even a golden pilsner can add flavour, zestiness and texture to any number of different sauces.

Desserts Beer is a marvellous addition to desserts. Good cooking is about balance – the bitter quality of a beer is the perfect foil for the sweetness of a rich chocolate tart. Ice creams, fruit coulis and sweet sauces can all benefit from the addition of an appropriate beer.

Lets get cooking

We can talk about different cooking methods for different dishes, and which beers to use, until we're blue in the face. But cooking is all about, well... cooking. So, when it comes to cooking with beer, don't be afraid to experiment; use different beers to the ones I've suggested, and don't be afraid to make mistakes – which can often turn into something more interesting and tasty anyway. You'll make your own unique discoveries and gain a catalogue of those mussel-like 'eureka' moments.

Par-cooking

This is a professional cooking technique, which I find surprisingly absent from most cookbooks. But it doesn't half make life easier, and generally does away with that head-scrambling, manic panic stage of 'timing everything so it's all ready at the same time', which seems to be an endemic fear amongst most aspiring home-cooks.

Essentially, it involves taking as much of the prep as possible to a point, one step away from finished, allowing to cool, and then storing it in the appropriate fashion until it's required for 'service'. For example, this may involve cooking a risotto until very al dente (with a firm bite), then cooling down as quickly as possible and refrigerating until required. All you would then do to serve, is heat it in a pan with an extra ladle of stock and stir in your other pre-prepared ingredients such as butternut squash purée and grated parmesan. Basically, this stage takes as long as it takes to get hot enough to serve. You also don't have the worry of messing it up in front of an expectant table of dinner party guests because you got the hard bit over with the day before in the privacy of your own kitchen. So, if you did screw up there's plenty of time to try again. This technique is particularly useful when serving up a full English breakfast: simply cook each ingredient i.e. bacon, sausage, tomato, black pudding to the point that a few minutes of further grilling or oven heat will render them ready, and set aside. Even poached eggs can be par-cooked, by simmering in acidulated water – and beer of course, until just firm enough to remove with a slotted spoon without falling apart, and then plunging straight into iced water. When they're required, simply lower into a pan of fresh, very hot water to warm through – which will also firm up the white just one more stage.

Vegetables are ideal for the par-cooking process. Beans, carrots and other veg you might boil can be cooked until al dente in well-salted water, and then immediately refreshed under cold running water until cool. They can then be drained and stored in the fridge until required. It's then a simple process of either plunging them into boiling water for just a couple of minutes, or tossing in a little butter and water, in a frying pan which gives them a vibrant glaze: most attractive for impressing at dinner parties.

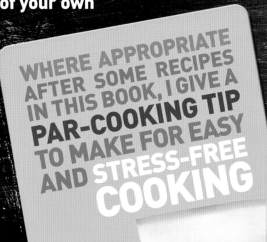

WHERE APPROPRIATE AFTER SOME RECIPES IN THIS BOOK, I GIVE A PAR-COOKING TIP TO MAKE FOR EASY AND STRESS-FREE COOKING

Breakfast

This may not be the most PC way to open a book in which beer plays such a dominant role. But indulge me. From a historical perspective, beer has been enjoyed as a breakfast beverage through, at least, Tudor and Elizabethan England; Queen Elizabeth I enjoyed a particularly large breakfast consumption, while in the 16th century, the Earl of Northumberland and his wife probably enjoyed at least a litre of beer with brekkie.

Obviously I'm not advocating setting off for work with this kind of intake – in fact with any intake, and we must bear in mind that the water at this time in history was far more likely to kill you than a lifelong beer-with-breakfast habit.

Having said all this, I am fanatical about the quality of my breakfast experience – particularly on those lazy Sunday mornings when chilling with friends is about as hectic as life becomes. And, on such Sundays, it's highly likely that you're going to have at least a few bottles or cans from the night before just hanging around with a few dregs of this and that. And believe me, those otherwise down the sink remains are going to add zest and a lift to all manner of breakfast delights – just be sure to check for stray cig butts before you start!

look out for the dregs

Toasted!

RISE & SHINE!

Breakfast

Baked Mexican Eggs

This is about as good as it gets for a post-party breakfast. Not only are you using up last nights dinner party menu left-overs, or footie-final food – but the dregs of the beer as well. The hot chilli will give you a morning kick-start to rival a large dose of Barrocca (amazing effervescent vitamin C tablets – if you haven't already tried them). You'll feel so fired-up and Latino after this, the only danger is you may just go and do yesterday's party all over again!

Method

Mix together the beer and the cream. Place the chilli in the bottom of a shallow, ovenproof dish and make a well in the middle. Break an egg into a small cup (in case of shell) and pour it into the well. Season the egg with salt and pepper and pour a tablespoon of the beer and cream mixture over the egg. Butter some silver foil and secure it over the top of the dish, making sure the foil isn't in contact with the top of the egg. Bake in a 180°C pre-heated oven for about 15 minutes – or until the egg white is set and the mince has warmed through.

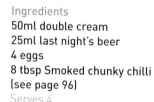

Ingredients
50ml double cream
25ml last night's beer
4 eggs
8 tbsp Smoked chunky chilli (see page 96)
Serves 4

Eggs en cocotte

This is a classic, luxury breakfast dish. Served up on a Sunday morning, on a tray – complete with red rose – it could just as easily fit into the romance and adventure category. Just make sure you've got plenty of toasted soldiers at the ready to mop everything up. Suitable beers for the cream mixture are going to be well-rounded, full-flavoured beers such as Old Speckled Hen, London Pride or Bishop's Finger.

Ingredients
2 eggs
2 rashers streaky bacon
25ml double cream
15ml beer
Makes 2

Method
Butter 2 ramekins and season with salt and pepper. Grill the bacon on one side only, until crispy. Cut the bacon into a small dice and spread evenly on the bottom of each ramekin. Break an egg into each ramekin (break into a cup first in case of shell), season the top with salt and pepper and then pour a tablespoon of the cream and beer mixture over each one. Cover with foil and put them in a pan with water to come about half way up the ramekins. Bring the water to a simmer on the stove and then carefully transfer to a 180°C pre-heated oven. Bake for about 10 minutes – or until the white is set and the yolk is still soft. To serve, loosen the eggs from the sides of the ramekins with a knife and turn out onto a slice of toast – or dig in straight from the ramekin.

Breakfast

Eggs Benedict

The recipe given below is for a monster – 2 eggs and 2 muffin halves per person. But this is a true classic and without doubt, fulfils the old adage: 'breakfast like a king'. For a lighter weight breakfast, just halve the ingredients.

Ingredients
4 spoonfuls of Hollandaise sauce (see Hollandaise recipe page 24)
4 eggs
2 muffins
4 slices ham
100g baby spinach
Splash of white wine vinegar
Oil and butter for frying
Serves 2

Method
Bring a pan of water, with a good slug of white wine vinegar to a gentle simmer. When you're ready to cook the eggs, give it a gentle swirl with a whisk or fork and carefully add the eggs.

The swirling action of the water helps to keep the white wrapped around the yolk, giving them a nice oval shape. Halve the muffins to give 4 round discs and then toast them. Lay a piece of ham on each half. Heat a pan with a dessert spoon of veg oil and a little knob of butter and add the washed and de-stalked spinach, season with salt and pepper and wilt – this only takes a couple of minutes. Drain off any excess water, and then gently squeeze out any residual liquid by wrapping the spinach in a clean tea-towel. Divide the spinach between the 4 muffin bases. When the eggs are cooked, remove them with a slotted spoon, dry carefully on some kitchen paper or clean tea towel and sit them on the spinach. Season the eggs, top with the Hollandaise and serve immediately.

PAR-COOKING TIP

POACHED EGGS CAN BE PREPARED IN ADVANCE TO AVOID LAST MINUTE PANIC BROUGHT ON BY MISJUDGED TIMINGS OR BROKEN YOLKS. SIMPLY POACH THE EGGS AS ABOVE, BUT A MINUTE OR SO BEFORE YOU WOULD NORMALLY TAKE THEM OUT OF THE PAN TO SERVE, TAKE OUT AND PUT INTO A BOWL OF ICED WATER. THEY CAN BE KEPT LIKE THIS UNTIL REQUIRED. THEN, HEAT A PAN OF FRESH WATER UNTIL IT'S HOT BUT NOT BOILING. THEN, AS YOU PLATE UP THE BREAKFAST, HEAT THE EGGS THROUGH IN THE HOT WATER AND DRAIN AS ABOVE.

Breakfast

Hollandaise Sauce

The textbook method for making Hollandaise involves messing around with reductions, and all manner of herbal adjuncts that you may or may not have in. This is my quick method, where the addition of wheat beer more than makes up for the short cuts. Once made, keep it in a warm place until required, but don't attempt to reheat otherwise you risk splitting it. If it does split however, just try whisking in a few drops of cold water, which, most of the time, brings things back together.

Ingredients
2 egg yolks
Juice of ½ a lemon
1 tbsp Berliner Weiss bier,
such as Paulaner or try
O'Hanlon's Double Champion
1 dsp white wine vinegar
250g butter
Serves 6

Method
Heat the butter gently in a saucepan until it's melted and a white foam forms on the top.

Remove from the heat and leave to stand for a couple of minutes. With a dessertspoon, carefully scrape the white foam off the top leaving behind clear golden butter. When most of this foam is removed, carefully pour the clear liquid into a small jug leaving behind any white residue in the bottom of the pan.

Set a heatproof bowl over a pan of simmering water and add the egg yolks, lemon, beer, vinegar and seasoning. Whisk the mixture until it goes light and fluffy, and begins to thicken. Remove from the heat, and add the warm butter – a few drops at a time at first, and then in a slow stream, whisking all the time. The Hollandaise should be smooth and yellow and of a thick, pouring consistency. If it splits, try whisking in a few drops of cold water to re-amalgamate.

Breakfast

Poached salmon scrambled eggs

If I'm passionate about my breakfast experience, then I'm positively obsessed when it comes to the quality of my scrambled eggs. I can recall being served a smoked salmon and scrambled egg bagel at some trendy party in an over-priced London hotel: the scrambled eggs were over-cooked and under-seasoned – and goodness knows what some poor sap had been charged for this culinary travesty. I was struck with incredulity that a trained chef in one the most prestigious hostelries in the world could put out a plate of such bland, poorly prepared food. Maybe his terrine of crayfish set in aspic is a work of art – but if you can't cook an egg...? okay, that's my rant over with now – every cook book should have one!

Ingredients
2 slices of toast
100g salmon fillet – skinned
60ml wheat beer
60ml water
dill and parsley stalks
(optional)
1 slice lemon
2 star anise
10g unsalted butter
4 eggs
25ml double cream
2 tsp chopped chives
Salt and pepper
Serves 2

Method
Place the salmon in a small pan and cover with the beer and water. Add the lemon, star anise and herb stalks. On a low heat bring the pan up to a slow simmer and then immediately turn off the heat. Leave the salmon in the pan for ten minutes with the poaching liquid, and then remove and allow to cool. When cool, flake the salmon into pieces.

To make the scrambled eggs, melt the butter over a gentle heat and add the beaten, seasoned eggs. When almost cooked i.e. loose and very slightly runny, add the flaked salmon followed by the double cream – which stops the cooking process. Add the chopped chives. Heat for another 10 seconds or so, and serve immediately on hot, buttered toast.

Gordon the guru goes to work on an egg!

Boiled egg with Welsh rarebit soldiers and Pancetta salt

A perfectly cooked boiled egg (runny yolk, firm white) and toasted soldiers is one of those food experiences that we never grow out of. It's a rejuvenating moment when the pressures and strains of adult life give way to carefree childhood memories from the very first dip. The Welsh rarebit and pancetta just serve to give it an added, adult, air of luxury, without taking away from its timeless simplicity.

Ingredients
2 eggs
1 slice of pancetta
2 slices Welsh rarebit
(see page 101)
Serves 2

Method
Put the pancetta on kitchen parchment paper, on a baking sheet. Put in a 180°C pre-heated oven for 15 minutes or until crispy. Allow to cool before crumbling. Put the eggs in a large pan of boiling water. Return to the boil and simmer for 5$\frac{1}{2}$ minutes for a medium egg – runny yolk, firm white. While the eggs cook, grill the Welsh rarebit until golden brown. Sprinkle the pancetta onto the plate, slice the rarebit into soldiers and dip away!

Breakfast

Dutch breakfast with Porter poached egg

This breakfast is pretty much responsible for everything that's happened to me since the age of 20. Let me explain: a college lecturer – rather recklessly – sent me off to Amsterdam at the age of 19 on my Catering College industrial placement (albeit at my begging and pleading for that destination).

At the time I left England you couldn't get in a pub before 11.00am, let alone enjoy a perfectly cooked breakfast of fresh ingredients, reading the morning papers watching the world go by from a pavement table. So, when I experienced my first Dutch 'Eitzemeiter' breakfast of sliced ham, melted cheese and poached eggs – IN A BAR, at 9.00am, I was pretty much moved to tears, and it certainly defined my view of the way forward for pubs in the UK.

My beer of choice for this dish is a hearty, robust and tinglingly bitter porter, such as the marvellous London Porter from Fullers. A dash in the egg poaching water instead of vinegar seems to perform the same coagulating function, whilst adding an extra dimension to the poached egg.

Ingredients and method
Simply toast the bread and spread on the butter; lay on a slice or two of quality ham (carved off the bone would be good); add some thinly sliced cheddar and bang under the grill until the cheese melts and starts to blister. Meanwhile, bring about 200ml of water to the simmer with about 100ml of Porter. Give it a swirl with a fork or whisk and gently lower in the egg. Cook as described for 'Eggs Benedict' and put on top of the melted cheese, season and imagine a languid summer in old Amsterdam.

Fruit salad with strawberry beer crème fraîche

This is a truly awesomely healthy, daily power breakfast for the whole family – and it contains beer! But before you start writing to me about drink-driving or encouraging under-age drinking: all the alcohol gets boiled off in its preparation to leave a fragrant strawberry syrup to stir into the crème fraîche. Although the preparation of all this fruit can take a little time, once it's done, it just sits in the fridge for days developing even more flavour.

Ingredients
1 small pineapple
2 oranges
1 banana
1 apple
Juice of 1 lime
2 kiwi fruit
½ melon of your choice
75g strawberries*

Strawberry beer crème fraîche (see page 81 for raspberry variation)
Makes a few days' worth of fruity breakfast
*The fruit beers, raspberry, cherry and strawberry are interchangeable here, according to availability and your taste.

Method
Remove the top and bottom from the pineapple, and then work around cutting off all the skin. Slice into 1-2 cm slabs and then cut into cubes. To prep the orange, remove the top and bottom and the cut away the skin and pith – and segment. Slice the banana, cut the apple into small chunks; same with the kiwi fruit and the melon; hull and cut the strawberries and mix the whole lot together with the lime juice (this will help stop discolouration of the apple). Job's a good un'!

Amy gets fraîche!

No rest 'til bedtime!

Snackettes (canapés if we're being posh) for parties, snacks and sarnies for lunch or dinner – it's all here. Whether it's a few friends round for a screening of your latest holiday vid, or a house-and-a-half-full of party people with decks and dancin' – a few choice snackettes and some top beer are guaranteed to give a full-flavoured edge to any do. We're not talking about twee, finger-in-the-air, aspic-clad affectations either. Oh no, these are more full-monty, double-bite portions. Not only does this give us the all important flavour factor, but also allows for the benefits and wizardry of a dinner party, but without the need for a dining space, and most importantly, washing-up! Also, with loads of different beers flying around, there are always going to be some fab food sensations to match a beer. Many of these snackettes can be adjusted size-wise to fit into the pre-party, or non-party snack category, while vice versa is also true.

As far as sarnies go, I've spent years working out how to reduce a full-on, three-component-part meal into something which requires no cutlery, is outrageously quick to prepare and comes in that hotel, late-night, room service fantasy package, that is the club sandwich – the one-stop, all-purpose, anytime of the day meal. So, use this whole section as an ideas board: a source of inspiration for day-to-day, party-to-party, gastro-living. And while you're thinking about it: dash, splash and pour yourself round the kitchen like a demented beer chef, using up every last morsel of food and dreg of beer to create your own culinary magic.

sarnies

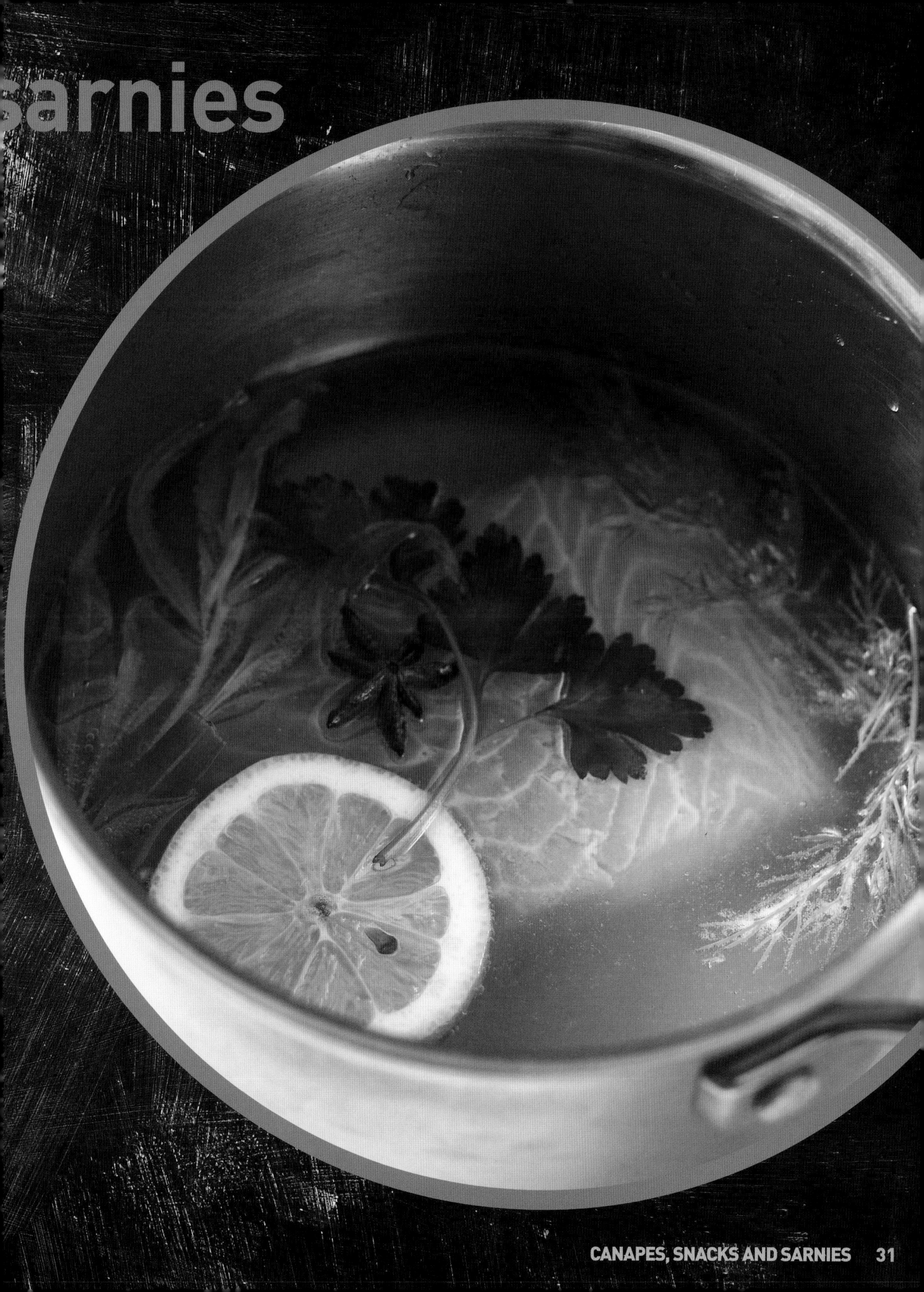

Canapés, snacks and sarnies

Mini Yorkshires with venison and raspberry beer jus

This is about as good as finger food can ever get: crunchy-topped, beer-infused Yorkshires; local meat – it could be lamb, beef, pigeon or sausage, and a rich gravy soaking into the whole thing – delicious! These mini Yorkshires are effectively edible vessels for just about anything you choose to put in them. You can even do veggie versions with left-over mash and baby roast vegetables. And just to keep true to origins, I'd recommend a good Yorkshire ale such as Black Sheep or Timothy Taylor's for the genuine northern experience.

Ingredients
50ml Yorkshire beer
250ml full fat milk
125g plain flour
3 eggs
Pinch of salt
Vegetable oil
50ml Raspberry beer
50ml beef or chicken gravy/jus
450g venison centre fillet
1 bunch watercress
Olive oil for frying
Makes about 18 mini Yorkshires

Method
First make the Yorkshire pudding batter mix: sift the flour and salt into a bowl and make a well. Break in the eggs and add half the milk. Whisk the mixture until it forms a smooth paste. Whisk in the remainder of the milk, and then the beer. Finally, pass through a fine sieve to remove any lingering lumps. Cover the mixture and refrigerate for at least 30 minutes before using. You can make the mixture a day in advance if you wish – but just be sure to give it a good stir – or whisk - before using.

When you're ready to make the dish, pre-heat the oven to 220°C. Put your Yorkshire pudding tray in the oven for five to ten minutes, then remove and pour a thin film of vegetable oil into the bottom of each recess. Put back in the oven for a couple of minutes to get really hot (almost smoking). Remove from the oven again and pour the batter mixture up to the rim in each recess, and carefully put back into

the oven. Leave for about fifteen minutes – or until the Yorkshires have risen and are brown and crispy around the top. (Resist the temptation to keep opening the oven door to check on progress, as this will prevent a good rise).

While the Yorkshires are cooking, you can pan-fry the venison: season the loin with salt and pepper; heat a frying pan over the hob, and then add a couple of dessertspoons of olive oil. Make sure the oil is nearly smoking hot before adding the venison. Fry until golden brown on all sides, remove from the pan and place on a tray in the oven for about five minutes – to achieve medium-rare. Remove from the oven and rest for at least five minutes before carving into thin slivers.

Meanwhile, put the pan you fried the venison in back on the hob, over a gentle heat, and add the raspberry beer – stirring to get all the residual venison flavours from the bottom of the pan. Add the gravy and allow to bubble for a minute or two before removing from the heat. To serve, put a sliver or two of venison in each Yorkshire, add a teaspoon of the raspberry gravy and garnish with a sprig of watercress.

PAR COOKING TIP
BAKE THE YORKSHIRES A DAY IN ADVANCE, AND THEN FREEZE. WHEN YOU'RE READY TO SERVE THE DISH, JUST TAKE THE YORKSHIRES STRAIGHT FROM THE FREEZER AND PUT IN A 200°C PRE-HEATED OVEN FOR ABOUT TEN MINUTES TO HEAT THROUGH. WHILE THIS IS HAPPENING YOU CAN COOK THE VENISON AND GRAVY AS ABOVE.

NOTE
FOR MINI YORKSHIRES, YOU CAN USE A TARTLET TIN, WITH HOLES OF APPROX 6CM IN DIAMETER.

Canapés, snacks and sarnies

Smoked aubergine and little gem boats

This is my beery version of the classic middle-eastern version of a dish called Babaganoush. It's a deliciously smoky humous-type dip, but with a truly unique preparation method which involves sticking the whole aubergine straight onto an open gas flame. Unfortunately, electric is no substitute. However, for about twenty quid, you can buy a little portable butane-powered hob from just about any outdoor/camping equipment shop. They're the business for any sort of picnic or al fresco dining – and a great barbecue supplement for heating sauces etc.

Ingredients
2 Aubergines
Beer – enough to cover the aubergine. (A strong, dark ale such as Morroco from The Daleside Brewery)
2 tsp light Tahini
4 tsp chopped parsley
2 small cloves garlic, crushed
100g goat's cheese
salt and pepper

4 baby gem lettuce
1 large baguette
Makes about 12 boats

Method
Pierce each aubergine with a fork, inserting the prongs all the way into the flesh about twelve times for each one. Cover with a full-flavoured English ale and leave overnight. To cook, dry the aubergine and place directly in an open flame allowing the skin to blacken and blister before turning. Once the whole skin is blackened and blistered, remove from the flame and allow to cool. This open flame method gives a fabulous smoked flavour to the flesh. The only down-side is the mess it makes of your gas hob. However, it will scrub up easily with a little hot water and washing-up liquid.

Once the flesh has cooled enough to handle, flake off the black skin. Squeeze out any excess liquid. After draining, chop up the flesh and combine with the tahini, lemon juice, garlic and seasoning. Crumble in the goat's cheese and refrigerate until required.

Separate the Cos leaves, wash and dry. Reserve the smaller, crisper inner leaves for this dish. Cut the baguette lengthwise though the middle, giving two halves. With a dessert spoon, scoop out the bread leaving a boat shaped shell. Reserve the scooped out bread for bread crumbs for another recipe. Liberally drizzle olive oil over the inner surface of the bread boats, season with salt and pepper and place in a 180°C pre-heated oven for about 6 minutes. Remove from the oven and set aside until required. To assemble, line the bread boats with the Cos leaves, and then spoon in the aubergine mixture. You can then cut them into short lengths and arrange on a serving platter (right).

Canapés, snacks and sarnies

Grilled goat's cheese pesto on crostini

Why bother with some insipid-looking manufactured stuff that looks as though someone's stuffed the contents of last week's lawn-mower cuttings in a jar, when you can knock up your own vibrant creation in minutes. The goat's cheese is an optional extra, which can give it a point of interest, bulk it out and make it more of a bruschetta topping than if just left in its pure form. The combination of such individually powerful flavours in the pesto requires a beer of equal power and complexity to stand up to it. A Belgian Tripel will fit the bill perfectly – however, with abv's around the 8% mark, consume in moderation!

Famous Belgians!

Ingredients
1 clove garlic
30g pine nuts
100g basil (after main, thick stalks removed)
1 dsp beer (a Belgian Tripel such as Westmalle or Leffe)
50ml olive oil
30g freshly grated Parmesan
60g goat's cheese (skin removed)

Small baguette, ½ cm slices
Makes about 20 crostinis

Method
To make the pesto: lightly toast the pine nuts in a 180°C pre-heated oven until they go light brown – this only takes a few minutes, so keep a close eye. Remove and allow to cool. Put the pine nuts, garlic, basil and beer in a food processor and blitz while gradually pouring in the olive oil. Add the Parmesan and then crumble in the goat's cheese. Cover and refrigerate.

To make the crostini: slice the baguette as thinly as possible into discs. Lay them out in a single layer on an oven tray and drizzle with olive oil, and then season with sea salt and freshly ground black pepper. Place in a 180°C pre-heated oven for six or seven minutes – or until light brown around the edges. Keep checking them, as they turn from perfect to over-done in seconds. Store them in an airtight container at normal room temperature.

Cheesy beer balls (profiteroles)

Mention pastry to most professional chefs, let alone the aspiring home cook and it induces cold sweats, worry, and general all-over nervousness. Applied to the skilled art of making filo or puff, that's totally understandable, but choux is so simple you could get the kids to do it. In this recipe, beer is substituted for water – it's a no-brainer really! For an extra bit of canapé life luxury, pipe in the Roquefort cheese mixture recipe from page 90.

Ingredients
125ml beer (just about any good British ale)
30g butter
75g plain flour
Pinch of salt
30g grated cheddar
2 eggs
Makes about 30 bite-size balls

Method
Pre-heat the oven to 180°C. Heat the beer in a pan. Add the butter and melt. Add the flour and salt and beat until the mixture forms into a smooth ball. Remove from the heat and add one egg and beat until amalgamated. Add the second egg and mix again. The mixture should be smooth and shiny. Using a teaspoon or dessertspoon – depending on how big you want the finished profiteroles – spoon the mixture onto a buttered baking sheet and place at the top of the oven for 10 minutes. After 10 minutes of baking – or until they're golden brown and crispy on top, open the oven door and leave for another 10 minutes. The profiteroles can now be filled with a filling of your choice.

Welsh rarebit triangles with soft boiled quails egg

If you're going to serve this one to a room full of vertical drinking guests, make sure you make ten times more than you think you'll need because they'll disappear off the serving plate before you've traversed the first 3 yards of the room....again, again, and again!

Ingredients
16 quails eggs
4 slices of bread
250g mature cheddar, grated
50ml beer
2 egg yolks
1 level tsp English mustard powder
A few drops of Worcester sauce

Method
If you have a food processor, blitz all the ingredients, except the bread and the quails eggs to a paste. In the meantime, toast the bread on both sides. When ready to serve, spread the mixture over each piece of toast in a thick, even layer, making sure you cover right up to the edges. Put under a pre-heated grill until the cheese browns and starts to blister. Cut each slice of toast into 4 triangles, top with a soft boiled quails egg and serve.

PREP TIP

TO PREPARE THE QUAILS EGGS, SIMPLY PLUNGE INTO BOILING WATER FOR EXACTLY 21/2 MINUTES – YOU'LL NEED HALF AN EGG PER TRIANGLE. THEN IMMEDIATELY PUT UNDER COLD RUNNING WATER UNTIL COOL. SHELL, CUT IN HALF AND PLACE ON TOP OF EACH RAREBIT TRIANGLE. SEASON THE HALVED EGGS WITH A LITTLE SEA SALT AND FRESHLY GROUND PEPPER.

PAR COOKING TIP

MAKE THE TOAST, SPREAD OVER THE MIXTURE AS DESCRIBED, AND THEN FREEZE. WHEN YOU WANT TO SERVE, SIMPLY PRE-HEAT THE GRILL AND PUT THE FROZEN RAREBIT UNDER THE GRILL. IT WILL DEFROST WHILE IT GRILLS GIVING YOU PERFECT RESULTS.

Canapés, snacks and sarnies

Slow roast belly pork, apple sauce and black pudding bruschetta

This is the perfect way to use up any excess belly pork left over from the slow cooked recipe on page 67. I reckon the combination of melt-in-the-mouth belly pork, apple sauce and black pudding is one of the world's greatest food combos. I also defy anyone to come up with a wine that's as good as an accompaniment as a French bière de Garde such as Saint Sylvestre, or Saison Dupont from southern Belgium. Go for anything from a bite-size canapé version turning the baguette into crostini (see page 36), to full length baguette for the ultimate open sarnie experience.

Ingredients
Belly pork (see page 67)
Baguette
one cooking bramley
1 tsp caster sugar
Black pudding

Method
Firstly make the apple sauce: peel, quarter and de-core the apples, cut into a dice and then place in a saucepan with the sugar and a teaspoon of water. Cook gently for about 10 minutes on a low heat until the apples just start to collapse, but still retain the smallest amount of 'bite'. One apple will yield enough sauce for about 4 bruschettas. Slice the black pudding and fry in a little oil for a couple of minutes on each side. In the meantime, heat a few slices of the belly pork in a 180°C pre-heated oven, Sit the pork slices in a couple of tablespoons of stock or water to prevent the meat drying out. Heat until just warmed through. In the five minutes it takes to heat the pork, slice the baguette on a slight bias into slices about 1 1/2 cm thick. Sprinkle with olive oil, sea salt and freshly ground pepper, and lightly toast on both sides. To serve, simply pile some belly pork on each slice of toasted baguette, add a dollop of apple sauce and top with a slice of black pudding. Don't forget to offer a bowl of crackling – if you haven't already eaten it all!

Poached salmon, mixed green leaf, with lemon and dill yoghurt dressing club sandwich

This feels like a truly indulgent and luxurious lunchtime experience – and therefore one we couldn't possibly afford the time to prepare, or have the audaciousness to eat in the office while everyone else is tucking into their plasti-clad tuna and cucumber. The reality is: it's not expensive on ingredients, takes minutes to prepare – and why not afford yourself a little treat in the midst of the daily slog.

Ingredients and Method
I favour a quality crusty whole white loaf with that wonderful dusting of flour, which, even if bought from a supermarket, is still reminiscent of some long-lost artisan bakery. For the dill and yoghurt dressing, just squeeze a little lemon juice into plain yoghurt and add chopped dill. Poach the Salmon accoring to the recipe on page 26. Once the salmon is cooked and cool, just flake it into a bowl and add a little dressing to bind it all together. Two final bonuses: this is an awesomely healthy sandwich, and light enough not to induce the usual bout of post-lunch slumber.

Pigeon and caramelised onion club sandwich

This is top tasting, beer soaking, footie friendly fodder of the highest order. Made in minutes, eaten in less, and not a utensil in sight. If you want to be really 'cheffy' about it then buy whole pigeons, remove the breasts and save the carcasses for a fabulous gamey stock: Just brown the carcasses in the oven, then place in a pan and just cover with water. Add a few bits of carrot, onion and celery, and then simmer for half an hour or so. Strain the liquid and add it to regular chicken stock for extra, gamey flavour. This food goes with just about any beer – but with a fruit beer on offer you'll get a great interplay of flavours, and any non-beer loving girls will be converted on their first sip. Game on.

Ingredients
4 pigeon breasts
8 rashers of bacon

marinade
50ml olive oil
100ml Kriek
2 sprigs thyme
2 cloves garlic
2 small onions (finely sliced)
Knob butter
1 tbsp veg oil
Serves 4

Method
Mix the marinade ingredients together and marinate the pigeon breasts overnight. To prepare the sandwiches, heat the oil and butter in a frying-pan, add the onions and fry until golden brown. Add the pigeon marinade to the onions, and cook for a couple of minutes until they take on a jammy consistency. Dry the pigeon breasts on kitchen paper, and then season with salt and pepper on both sides. Fry skin side down for a couple of minutes and then turn and fry for another minute. Transfer the breasts to an ovenproof tray and place in a 180ºC pre-heated oven for 5 mins. Pour 100ml water into the pan in which you fried the pigeon breasts and bring to the boil – stirring vigorously to get the flavours off the bottom of the pan. Add the onion mixture and keep warm. While the pigeons are resting after removing from the oven, grill the bacon, make 3 slices of toast per person, and put a layer of onions on 4 slices of toast. Slice the pigeon breasts thinly and arrange on the onions. Put another piece of toast on each pigeon and onion mix and then spread a layer of mustard mayo on each one. Add the salad leaves, the final slice of toast and cut each one into 4.

Get fruity!

Canapés, snacks and sarnies

Fish Finger club sandwich with coriander and beer mayo

I've always felt that fish fingers stand up gastronomically – and I've taken some stick as a result. Absolution finally arrived when the fish finger sandwich appeared on the menu at John Torode's Smiths of Smithfield. I was so excited at this discovery, I went away and created this monster version to celebrate! It's still one of my all-time favourite lunches.

Ingredients
3 slices of buttered bread
4 fish fingers
2 tbsp mayonnaise
(see page 87)
1 dsp chopped coriander
Handful of mixed salad leaves
30g frozen peas
Makes 1

Method
Cook the fish fingers according to the instructions on the packet, and do the same with the peas. Add the coriander to the mayonnaise. Put the fish fingers on one slice of bread. Put another slice of bread on the fish fingers and smother with mayonnaise. Spread over the peas, top with salad and the final slice of bread, also covered with mayonnaise. Cut in half and get stuck in.

New Orleans shrimp po boy

Well, this is more big juicy tiger-prawn than shrimp, but we should stick with the good ol' Orleans terminology for the sake of authenticity. The Po Boy is a New Orleans classic and a kind of baguette-with-battered-filling version of our Club sarnie. In other words, you can put in what the hell you like. The only stipulation is to batter the main ingredient, and apply ample quantities of mayonnaise. The rest is down to you, your imagination, and the contents of your fridge. A Louisiana favourite is made with deep fried oysters – a real treat, and well worth the time, effort and money.

Ingredients

For the batter
4 oz plain flour
1 tsp baking powder
1/2 tsp salt
150ml good English Ale
100ml water

320g uncooked tiger prawns, cleaned and de-veined
4 x 9" baguettes
Makes 4 x 9" sarnies

Method

To make the batter, put the flour, salt and baking powder in a mixing bowl. Add the beer and water and whisk until smooth. Allow to rest for 1 hour, uncovered.

To deep-fry, ideally use a thermostatically-controlled deep fat fryer. If you don't have one, bring a large pan of vegetable oil up to about 175ºC. It has reached this temperature when a cube of fresh bread will brown in about 1 minute. Be extremely careful as the oil will eventually catch fire if it gets too hot. When the oil is up to temperature, put the baguette in a 180ºC pre-heated oven to warm through. Dry the prawns well and lightly coat in seasoned flour, shaking off any excess. Dip in the batter and carefully lower into the hot oil. Deep-fry until golden brown – this only takes between thirty seconds and a minute. Drain well on kitchen paper. Keep warm in the oven while you cut the baguette and spread generously over the mayonnaise. Add any further fillings of your choice such as salad or gherkins add the prawns and tuck in, Louisiana-style.

BBQ

In my opinion, there are two defining rituals of civilised behaviour: siestas and al fresco dining. In an ideal world, the former would be sandwiched between the latter and performed on a daily basis. In reality, we have to wait for the onset of our, oh-so-short summer in order to snatch a few days of BBQ life. So, we should be doing everything possible to maximise the experience when it happens. Beer is as synonymous with BBQ food as the coals it's cooked on. But it's also fantastic when used as a marinating ingredient – BBQ's, by definition, can easily dry out food or leave it charred on the outside and uncooked in the middle. So anything that helps add a juicy tenderness should be welcomed with open arms.

Apart from beer, the secret of a successful barbie is to regard the BBQ structure itself as just a stage in the food preparation process, rather than the only possible cooking option – food can be par-boiled, baked or sautéed in the kitchen, in advance; a barbecued item can make up the final component part of a dish, while vegetables benefit the most from complete pre-cooking, with just a quick charring to finish on the barbie. Rather than make things harder, this should make life much less stressful – you've got back-up, and time, and it's not cheating. The whole experience should be about pleasure, not pain – and allow for ample sleep time in the afternoon before the guests come round.

"Let the boy coo

INDOOR BBQ TIP

THE DELICIOUS BBQ CHAR-GRILLED FLAVOUR, CAN EASILY BE SIMULATED INDOORS USING A RIDGED CAST-IRON GRILL PLATE (SHOWN RIGHT). JUST PLACE ON YOUR GAS HOB, HEAT UP FOR 10-15 MINUTES AND RE-CREATE THOSE SUMMER BARBIE FLAVOURS ON A RAINY NOVEMBER NIGHT.

she'll drink to that...

BBQ

Piri Piri Poussin

This is the kind of food barbecues were designed for – a bright red, fiery-as-hell chilli marinade; a refreshing, floral and buttery pilsner lager which acts as marinade ingredient, and a foil for the chilli heat, when drunk as the accompanying beverage. While chicken thighs can easily be burnt on the outside before they're cooked through in the middle, and breast can dry out really quickly – a poussin, if spatchcocked, (cut down the middle and cooked flat), and pre-cooked in the oven – is small enough to keep on the bone. This way, it will retain more moisture and flavour, and will chargrill and heat through at the same time.

Ingredients
2 Poussins
300g red chillies
25ml olive oil
Juice of 1 lemon
2 tsp smoked paprika
Pinch of salt
Black pepper
50ml pilsner lager
Serves 2

Method
To make the marinade, remove the stalks from the chillies and deseed ¾ of them. Combine all the ingredients, except the poussin, in a food processor and blend to a paste.

To prepare the poussin, turn it up-side-down. With a sharp, heavy knife cut it through the backbone. Split the poussin open and then cut through the breast bone to split into two identical halves. Make about three or four incisions into the legs and breasts of each of the four halves and rub the marinade all over, really working it in to every nook, crevice and cranny. Cover and refrigerate for 12 to 24 hours. To cook, simply roast in a 180°C pre-heated oven for about twenty minutes – or until the juices run clear when a skewer is inserted into the thigh. Finish on the BBQ for a few minutes on each side for that fabulous chargrilled flavour.

PAR COOKING TIP

HAVING TAKEN THE POUSSIN OUT OF THE OVEN ALLOW TO COOL, AND THEN REFRIGERATE. IT WILL KEEP PERFECTLY WELL FOR A FEW DAYS SO LONG AS THE POUSSIN IS REALLY FRESH. IN FACT THE LONGER IT STAYS IN THE MARINADE, THE MORE THE FLAVOURS WILL INFUSE AND DEVELOP. JUST CHARGRILL OR BBQ TO SERVE.

Stuffed steak with beer marinated cheese

We're after retaining moisture and succulence here, while adding variety and originality to the usual suspects. We've also brought together three ingredients that represent one of food and drink's most desirable 'ménages à trois:' steak, cheese and beer. As far as the marinating beer goes, you can pretty much use whatever you've got in, but I would always favour a malty, hoppy English ale for a steak and cheese dish such as Bishop's Finger from the excellent Shepherd Neame brewery.

Ingredients

4 sirloin steaks (about 2^1/$_2$ cm thick)
160g mature cheddar, finely grated
4 tsp whole grain mustard
Several drops of Worcester sauce
100ml beer

Serves 4

Method

Mix together the cheese, mustard, Worcester sauce and beer. With a sharp, pointed knife, make a lateral incision in the side of the steak. Proceed to make a pocket inside the steak and stuff the cheese mixture into it. Try to keep the entrance hole as small as possible, and the pocket as large as possible without piercing the surface or other edges of the steak. Secure the opening with half a cocktail stick that's been soaked in water – which prevents it from burning. Just before cooking, season the steak with salt and pepper, brush with oil and barbecue or char-grill until cooked to your liking.

BBQ

Sausage and mash burger

Sausage and mash cooked on the barbie? "Surely the mash would fall through the grill" my mate Simon hilariously remarked. "Not so" said I, "not when the mash is encased in a herby, juicy minced pork pattie". Not only does the mash ooze out in a molten, buttery way when you cut into it, but it prevents the classic barbie problem of drying out burgers, or leaving them raw in the middle. While a good malty, hoppy English ale is a perfect foil for the sweetness of the pork as an ingredient – and also ideal if you're serving this one up as winter comfort food – I would advocate a refreshing, cleansing pilsner or dry Belgian Abbaye beer for a summer barbie.

Ingredients
180g beer mash
(see page 73)

600g minced pork
1 small onion, finely chopped
3 cloves garlic, crushed
1 dsp chopped parsley
1 dsp chopped sage
30g fresh breadcrumbs
salt and pepper to taste
75ml beer, such as Timothy Taylor's 'Landlord'
1 egg
Makes 4 hefty burgers

Method
Make the burger mix by simply combining all the ingredients, except the mash, and then refrigerate the mixture. The mash should also be well refrigerated, as it's much easier to handle when cold and firm. When you're ready to assemble, divide the pork mixture into eight and make a well in the middle of each one. Divide the mash equally between four of the patties pressing it into the well. Place another Pattie on top of each mash-filled one and seal around the edges, shaping into a burger as you do. To cook, simply brush with oil and barbecue in the usual manner.

GARLIC TIP

REMOVE THE ROOT FROM INSIDE THE GARLIC CLOVE AS IT CAN CAUSE INDIGESTION AND BE BITTER. ALSO, SPRINKLE SALT OVER THE GARLIC AND LEAVE FOR A FEW SECONDS BEFORE CRUSHING, AS THIS HELPS BREAK IT DOWN MORE EASILY.

BBQ

Halloumi & Mushrooms with roast tomato coulis

There are not many cheeses you can throw straight on the BBQ without them causing total meltdown. Halloumi is one of them – possibly the only. It transforms itself from old, school rubber to soft and tasty gastro fodder in minutes. Together with the mushroom, pesto and tomato coulis you've got a vegetarian medley worthy of the finest dining table, let alone a rustic summer barbie. Rather bizarrely, Belgian 'Tripel' beers – that's the REALLY strong ones – go great with the big pesto flavours.

Ingredients
9 tsp of pesto (see page 36)
9 large flat cup mushrooms
3 packs Halloumi cheese
Bunch of thyme
3 cloves garlic
65g butter

For the roast tomato coulis
260g vine tomatoes
1 red pepper
25ml strong Belgian beer
of your choice
Makes 9

'Don't try this at home – use tongs'

everything for the fun-guy

Method

Make the coulis by placing the tomatoes and pepper on a baking tray, season with sea salt, freshly ground pepper and olive oil. Roast in a 180°C pre-heated oven for about 45 minutes. Remove from the oven and immediately place the red pepper in another container and cover with cling film. Leave to cool and then remove the skin from the peppers. Remove the seeds from the pepper. Blitz the tomato and pepper with a hand blender or in a food processor with the beer, then pass it through a fine sieve and correct the seasoning. Cover and refrigerate. Peel and remove the stalks from the mushrooms and arrange in a single layer on a baking tray – use two trays if necessary. Dot the mushrooms with the butter, finely slice the garlic and sprinkle over. Add the sprigs of thyme and then season with sea salt and freshly ground pepper. Loosely cover with kitchen foil and bake in a 180°C pre-heated oven for about 20 minutes. Remove from the oven, uncover and allow to cool. When you're ready to serve, slice each piece of Halloumi into 3 rectangular slabs and place directly on the BBQ. Turn when golden brown and BBQ the other side. At the same time, place the mushrooms on the BBQ. To serve, simply sit a mushroom on top of each piece of Halloumi, put a tsp of pesto on the mushroom and garnish with the roast pepper coulis.

BBQ

BBQ sauce

There are certainly no hard and fast rules when it comes to BBQ sauces – just let your creativity and personal preferences fly. If ever there was a time when you can give it the 'bit of this and a dash of that' routine, making a BBQ sauce is it. If you can get hold of a German smoked beer, then that would be a real treat – both as ingredient and accompaniment.

Ingredients
2 tbsp olive oil
1 onion, finely diced
1 small celery stick, finely sliced
2 cloves garlic, finely chopped
1 dsp chilli powder
1 dsp cumin powder
1 tsp smoked paprika
2 dsp tomato purée
125ml strong, fruity beer
125ml water
150ml tomato ketchup
1 dsp Worcester sauce
25ml white wine vinegar
Salt and pepper to taste
Makes about 750ml of sauce

Method
Heat the oil in a heavy-based saucepan. Add the onion, celery and garlic and cook gently for several minutes until soft. Add the chilli powder, cumin and smoked paprika and cook for a couple more minutes, stirring well. Add the tomato purée and cook for a couple more minutes. Add the remaining ingredients, stir well and simmer for about 20 minutes. Remove from the heat and blend to a smooth sauce. Cool and serve.

Girls just wanna have BBQ fun

Lamb Tagine skewers

A traditional, honey-and-lemon-infused, Moroccan Tagine is one of my all-time favourite dishes to cook and eat – it's an amazing case of taste over effort. Bursting with fragrant herbs and spices, and a perfect of balance of sweetness versus acidity from the addition of honey and lemon, this is the barbecue version that still captures all the classic elements. As far as the beer goes, honey has been added to beer since the earliest civilisations, so any decent honey-infused beer is the perfect complement both in, and with this dish. Fuller's Honey Dew is one of the best and most widely available.

Ingredients
400g lamb neck fillet, trimmed and cut into 2$^{1}/_{2}$ cm cubes
40ml olive oil
Big pinch of saffron strands
100ml honey beer
1 tsp turmeric
1 tsp cinnamon
1 tsp ground coriander
1 tsp ground ginger
2 cloves garlic
Zest and juice of 1 lemon
1 Aubergine
2 onions
Makes 4 skewers

Method

Finely chop one of the onions and crush or finely chop the garlic. Heat a couple of tablespoons of olive oil and gently fry the onions and garlic until they soften. Add the turmeric, cinnamon, coriander and ginger and fry, stirring regularly for a couple of minutes. Then add the lemon juice, honey, olive oil and saffron. Remove from the heat and blend the marinade in a food processor or with a hand blender. Allow to cool before mixing it with the cubes of lamb. Coat the meat well, cover and refrigerate, allowing the meat to marinate for at least twelve hours, preferably 24 hours. When you're ready to assemble the skewers, spread the meat out on a baking tray in a single layer, season with salt and pepper and cook in a 160°C pre-heated oven for about 40 minutes. Meanwhile cut the aubergine into $2^1/2$ cm cubes and squeeze over a little lemon juice to prevent discolouration. Peel the onion and cut into quarters. Then separate each quarter into its individual layers. When the meat has cooked and rested until cool, alternate on each skewer the meat, and aubergine making sure you've got a piece of onion or two between each piece of lamb and aubergine. The skewers can now be refrigerated until required for the BBQ or char-grill, when they'll heat through and get a lovely charred flavour – just turn every so often when they're nicely coloured on each side.

BBQ

Cheesy flat bread

This is the kind of thing that wins you friends and influences people!
Knocking up your own bread in minutes is the culinary equivalent of a
magician's sleight of hand – dead easy when you know how, but rocket
science if you don't. The thing with this flat bread is there's no proofing,
rising, yeast activity, knocking back or any of those mysterious practices
associated with bread making that seem more like chemistry than cooking.
And how you'll impress as you toss the rolled out dough on the barbie
while casually mentioning 'it's a little something I prepared earlier'.
It'll also go great with those lamb Tagine skewers (see page 52)
taking the beer and kebab concept to new culinary heights.

Ingredients
50g Brie
English ale, such as
Greene King's Abbot Ale,
to just cover the cheese
130g plain flour
50ml water
$^1/_4$ tsp baking
powder
$^1/_2$ tsp salt

Makes 6
pitta-sized
flat breads

Method
Cover the cheese completely
in the beer and leave for at least
5 days – the cheese will absorb
the beer and begin to break
down, which is what we want.

When you're ready to make
the actual breads, sift the flour,
salt and baking powder into a
food processor – or onto a work
surface if you don't have one.
Add the water and the drained
cheese (broken up into small
pieces if you don't have the
processor). Blitz for a few
seconds, or knead on the
work surface until you get
a smooth ball of dough. If
you're preparing this in a food
processor, you may still have
to knead it for a while on a
work surface to bring together
into a ball. Wrap in cling film
and refrigerate until required.
If you're cooking this on a char-
grill plate, get the plate really
hot before attempting to cook.
Divide the dough into 6 pieces
and roll out each piece on a
lightly floured work surface
until it's shaped into an oval
pitta shape. Try and roll them
out as thin as possible. Lay
straight on the BBQ or char-
grill plate for about 30 seconds
– or until it colours and blisters.
Turn and repeat. Serve warm.

PAR-COOKING TIP

ONCE ROLLED OUT, YOU CAN
LAYER UP THE UN-COOKED
BREADS BETWEEN LAYERS OF
KITCHEN PARCHMENT PAPER
AND TIGHTLY CLING FILM UNTIL
REQUIRED.

Life's a beach

Thai marinated swordfish

Wheat beer and marinated fish dishes are made for each other – particularly where South East Asian flavours are involved such as lemon grass, lime and coriander. Think of the ingredients, and proportions as just a guide – the wonderful thing about marinades is that you can let your imagination, and kitchen ingredients run the show. If you feel like throwing in some lemon zest – go for it; if you're missing an ingredient – fear not, experimentation is half the fun of cooking.

Ingredients
2 swordfish steaks

Marinade
150ml wheat beer, such as Hoegaarden
2 spring onions, finely sliced
1 tsp red chillies, finely sliced
1 clove garlic, finely sliced
1 tsp fresh ginger, finely chopped
Small bunch coriander
1 lime, juice and zest
Serves 2

Method
Mix all the marinade ingredients together and pour over the swordfish. Cover and refrigerate overnight. When ready to cook, pat the fish dry with kitchen paper, season with salt and pepper, brush with oil and barbecue until nicely browned on both sides, and only just cooked through.

BBQ

Pesto marinated monkfish and mushroom skewers with pancetta

There are not really many occasions when meat and fish combine together to good effect in the same dish, but the firm, white meaty flesh of the Monkfish is just fabulous with smoked pancetta – likewise, Scallops. Not only does the pancetta add fab flavour, but it also protects the fish from the drying powers of the BBQ, helping to keep it juicy and succulent. All manner of big flavoured beers will go well with this dish – from a powerful Belgian tripel to a German smoked beer.

Ingredients
300g trimmed Monkfish
8 medium-sized closed cup mushrooms
100g thin sliced pancetta
3 tbsp Pesto (see page 36)
10g butter
1 dsp olive oil
Makes 2 skewers

Method
Make the Pesto according to the recipe on page 36. but leave out the goat's cheese. Cut the Monkfish into 6 cubes about 3cm square. Coat with the pesto and set aside.

Brush the mushrooms clean and then fry in the oil and butter for a couple of minutes until lightly coloured and just cooked through. Set aside. If the skewers are wooden, make sure they've been soaked in water for at least half an hour to stop them burning. To assemble, slide on a mushroom, then a piece of Monkfish, then mushroom, then Monkfish, until you have 3 pieces of Monkfish and 4 mushrooms alternating on each skewer. Next, wrap a piece of pancetta tightly around each piece of Monkfish. You can now refrigerate the skewers until required for cooking. To cook, brush very lightly with oil and BBQ or chargrill for a couple of minutes on each side, or until the Monkfish is just cooked through.

BBQ Bananas

This is like BBQ'd banoffee pie!
– a classic combo of banana,
butterscotch sauce and
whipped cream.

Ingredients

4 bananas
90g unsalted butter
200g Demerara sugar
2 tbsp golden syrup
75ml double cream (plus more
for whipping)
1/4 tsp ground ginger
25ml Belgian tripel beer
200ml double cream, whipped
Serves 4

Method

First, make the sauce by heating the sugar and butter and golden syrup and cook gently until the sugar is dissolved. Add the cream and ginger and bring to the boil. Remove from the heat, cool, and only then, add the beer. Wrap the bananas individually in tin foil and place on the hot BBQ, turning occasionally. When the bananas are soft and hot in the middle (test them by inserting a fork or skewer), remove them, unwrap and slice lengthwise through the middle. Spoon over the caramel sauce and top with a dollop of whipped cream. These are delicious served with Old Speckled Hen which has a distinct banana aroma.

CHEERS!

Dinner party

The secret of successful dinner party entertainment is to keep it simple and use the highest quality produce you can get your hands on. By that, I don't mean extravagant ingredients like white Alba truffles or great mounds of Beluga from the Caspian Sea. I'm talking about Gloucester Old Spot Pork belly from the local butcher, seasonal English Asparagus and Orchard apples from Ampleforth (tended and picked by the monastery monks).

Stress-free entertaining

This is provenance-based, flavour-driven produce where nature and man have worked in perfect harmony to do virtually all the work for you. Perfunctory cooking will yield flavour to inspire conversation; even love and romance.

You can also forget about fancy presentation and fiddly garnishes, that may well look and taste great when delivered by the likes of Ramsay and Rhodes, but can all too easily wind up as a dog's dinner in lesser hands. So, let the ingredients do the talking; make life simple and stress free; apply some simple par-cooking techniques and don't, whatever you do, forget an artisan beer or two. Keep it real, and let the party commence.

Dinner party

Goat's cheese and butternut squash risotto

This is a great dinner party dish for a number of reasons (not least because of the taste). Risotto lends itself very well to the par-cooking process, giving you minimum cooking time prior to serving up to your guests. In addition, the sloppy nature of risotto means there's no fancy presentation to worry about – simply spoon it into bowl plates, garnish with chunks of roast squash, and you're into dinner party heaven. A light, zesty wheat beer not only adds a little fragrant luxury to the whole affair, but is also an ideal accompaniment.

Ingredients

400g risotto rice
1 onion, finely chopped
2 cloves of garlic, crushed
1 dsp chopped thyme
75ml olive oil
330ml wheat beer
1.5 litres chicken or veg stock
1 large butternut squash
75g unsalted butter
250g goat's cheese
75g freshly grated parmesan
Serves 4

PAR-COOKING TIP

MAKE THE PURÉE AND ROAST SQUASH UP TO A DAY BEFORE. COOK THE RISOTTO ACCORDING TO THE METHOD ABOVE UNTIL THE POINT OF BEING AL DENTE. IMMEDIATELY REMOVE FROM THE HEAT AND SPREAD OUT OVER A FLAT SURFACE IN ORDER TO COOL QUICKLY AND EVENLY. REFRIGERATE ALL THE COOKED INGREDIENTS UNTIL REQUIRED. TO SERVE, SIMPLY ADD A LADLE OF STOCK, OR WATER, TO A PAN, ADD THE RISOTTO AND HEAT THROUGH. WHEN IT'S HOT, ADD THE PURÉE, RE-HEAT THE CUBES IN THE OVEN, ADD THE GRATED PARMESAN AND SERVE.

Method

Peel the squash, and then cut in half length-wise. Scrape out the seeds from the bulbous end and slice this part into thin slices. Cut the remainder of the squash into approximately a 1cm dice. To make the purée, melt the butter in a heavy-based saucepan and add the sliced squash, gently cook for a few minutes and then add 150ml of the beer. Cook gently until the squash is very soft – this should take 20-25 mins. If the pan is going dry, just add a little water. When the squash is cooked, blend to a purée, add salt and pepper to taste, and set aside to cool.

While the purée is cooking, roast the cubes of squash in a 200°C pre-heated oven. Simply spread the squash on a baking tray in a single layer, season with salt and pepper, drizzle with olive oil and roast until tender, but not mushy (about 15-20 mins).

To make the risotto, bring the stock to a low simmer. In another, heavy-based saucepan, heat a tablespoon of olive oil and gently cook the onion, garlic and thyme until soft. Add the rice and stir for a couple of minutes. Add the remainder of the wheat beer and stir until nearly all the liquid has been absorbed. Add a couple of ladles of stock and stir until most of the liquid has been absorbed. Repeat this process until the rice is cooked to 'al-dente' (with a soft bite). This should take about 15 minutes. About 2-3 minutes before the rice is completely cooked, stir in the squash purée and crumble in the goat's cheese. Meanwhile, re-heat the squash cubes and add the parmesan to the risotto. To serve, garnish the risotto with the cubes of squash and some shaved fresh Parmesan. Serve with glasses of chilled wheat beer: delicious!

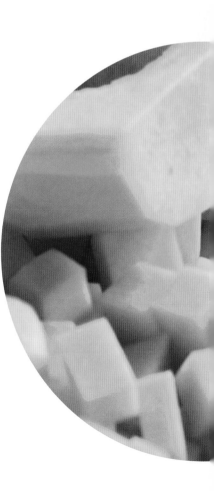

Dinner party

Prawn cocktail

This dish is making a big comeback and definitely fits into that Fondue-type, retro-cool category. But what takes this out of the Mateus Rose lamp holder era is the substitution of cucumber and avocado salad for the iceberg, and using fresh tiger prawns instead of little glazed frozen things. Throw in the home made Marie Rose and a glass of the 'oh-so-cool' wheat beer, and this old timer suddenly becomes cutting edge classic.

Ingredients
Avocado and cucumber salad (see page 97)
20 uncooked tiger prawns or langoustines
Wheat beer mayonnaise (see page 87)
1 dsp Tomato ketchup
Tabasco sauce
Pinch of paprika for garnish
Serves 4

Method
If the Prawns are still in their shells, remove the shell. Cut a slit down the back of the prawn and remove the – sometimes black – intestinal tract that runs along its back. Bring a pan of salted water to a simmer and add the prepared tiger prawns. Cook for about 30 seconds i.e. until just cooked through. Drain and set aside to cool. Mix the mayonnaise with the tomato ketchup and a few drops of Tabasco sauce. Divide the avocado and cucumber salad between the serving dishes of your choice. Pile on the prawns, spoon on the mayonnaise-based dressing (now – Marie Rose sauce) and serve. Garnish with whatever you like: wedge of lemon, tomato, paprika, etc – for that full retro vibe.

Pork Terrine

This classic country terrine is quite simply packed with flavour. It makes a perfect rustic opener to any dinner party, or picnic lunch. Garnishes of Cornichons (baby gherkins), a good piquant pickle and crusty bread are de rigueur. The big countryside flavours make it a perfect match for all manner of beers. It's as at home with a fruity English ale as it is with a farmhouse Belgian 'Saison'. In France, this dish would be known as Pâté de Campagne: so, if you want to keep the French theme, go for a Bière de Garde from Normandy. You can just use mince pork if you don't like the idea of veal or liver, just make the weight of meat up to a 1kg total.

Ingredients

750g streaky bacon
500g minced pork
250g minced veal
250g minced calves liver
1 onion, finely chopped
2 cloves of garlic, crushed
1 dsp chopped parsley
1 dsp chopped thyme
175ml of abbaye, trappist or similarly strong fruity beer
80g melted butter
Salt and pepper
Serve 8

Method

Pre-heat the oven to 160°C. Line a terrine dish (approximately 34cm long and 10cm wide) with the bacon, slightly overlapping to avoid any gaps. Combine all the remaining ingredients in a large bowl and mix together well. Spoon the mixture into the lined terrine dish, making sure you push it down into all the corners. Wrap over the overhanging bacon strips to form a sealed parcel and cover with kitchen foil. Place the terrine dish in a oven proof dish and add hot water to come about half way up the dish. Bring to a simmer on top of the stove and then transfer the whole thing to the oven for about an hour to an hour and a half. Check to see if it's cooked by inserting a skewer or knife into the middle of the terrine. The tip of the knife or skewer should be hot to touch, and the juices should run out clear.

Dinner party

Method
Blend all the base ingredients to a paste in a food processor. Heat a couple of tablespoons of olive oil in a heavy-based saucepan and gently fry the paste for 2-3 minutes, stirring all the time. Add the coconut milk; fill the empty coconut milk tin with water and add to the pan. Crumble in the stock cube and bring to the simmer stirring regularly. Simmer for about 20 minutes. Cook the noodles according to the instructions on the packet, drain and divide between four warmed bowl plates. Meanwhile, heat another heavy based saucepan, which

Seafood Laksa

This is quite simply, packed with flavour. The addition of a citrussy, herb infused wheat beer is a great twist to this Malaysian classic. Don't be put off by unfamiliar ingredients like palm sugar and shrimp cake (the pungent smell dissipates through cooking!): These more unusual ingredients are readily available through any Chinese supermarket – a visit is a fascinating culinary adventure in itself. The coriander and citrus notes in Belgian wheat beers lend themselves perfectly to these elements in the food.

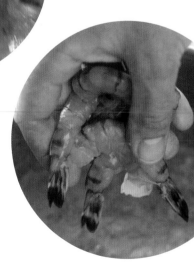

Ingredients

Laksa base
1/2 an onion, roughly chopped
25g coriander
3 sticks of lemon grass, tough outer skin removed, then roughly chopped
3 cloves garlic
25g fresh ginger
2 dsps turmeric powder
25g palm sugar
25g shrimp cake
20g red chillies

Olive oil for frying
500g live mussels
12 uncooked tiger prawns
400g Monkfish fillet
200ml Belgian wheat beer
1 tin coconut milk
1/2 chicken stock cube
200g egg noodles
A further handful of chopped coriander for garnish
Handful of bean sprouts
Serves 4

has a tight fitting lid. When the pan is good and hot, add the mussels and beer. Put on the lid and steam until the mussels are fully opened. This can be as quick as two minutes. Remove from the heat and set aside.

When the Laksa has completed its 20 minutes simmering time, add the Monkfish, and then 30 seconds later, the prawns. Simmer for a couple of minutes Add the mussels with all their cooking juice to the pan, and then the bean sprouts, and finally the chopped coriander. To serve, simply ladle the Laksa over the noodles and tuck in!

PAR-COOKING TIP

COOK THE LAKSA AS ABOVE, BUT REMOVE FROM THE HEAT AFTER THE 20 MINUTE SIMMER. COOL AND REFRIGERATE. COOK NOODLES ACCORDING TO THEIR INSTRUCTIONS, BUT REFRESH UNDER COLD, RUNNING WATER WHEN YOU REMOVE THEM FROM HEAT, THEN DRAIN. ADD A DESSERTSPOON OF OLIVE OIL AND REFRIGERATE. ALL THIS CAN BE DONE THE DAY BEFORE.

TO SERVE, HEAT THE LAKSA UNTIL JUST SIMMERING, BUT ADD THE NOODLES TO THE FINISHED LAKSA IN THE PAN AT THE LAST MINUTE, AND COOK THE FISH ACCORDING TO THE METHOD ABOVE.

Dinner party

'The sharper the knife
– the safer the knife'

Slow-cooked belly pork

The only way to cook belly pork is long and slow. Not only does
this make it melt-in-the-mouth tender, but also lends itself perfectly
to the addition of a full-flavoured, robustly strong Belgian or English ale,
where the beer flavours have got time to really penetrate and flavour the
meat. An abbaye ale such as Leffe blonde, Trappist such as Chimay, or full-
flavoured English ale such as Fullers 1845 are perfect. As far as presentation
goes, this is a gloriously rustic dish. So, rather than try and turn it into
something fancy, just stick a huge bowl of mash in the middle of the table;
pile the slices of pork on a big chopping board along with the ribs, and pour
all the sauce and veg into a soup tureen with ladle. Let everyone pile in
and decide their own proportions of mash to sauce to meat. If there are
any lingering doubts that a successful dinner party depends on twee towers
and sculptured garnishes, then this will banish them once and for all.

Ingredients
1 kg belly pork, preferably
with the bone still intact
2 carrots
1 stick celery
1/2 onion
3 cloves garlic
Fennel stalks (from 2 bulbs)
1 leek
300ml water
330ml beer
1/2 chicken stock cube
1 bay leaf
3 sprigs rosemary
1 tin chopped tomatoes

For the dry marinade:
1 dsp chopped Oregano
1 dsp chopped parsley
1 dsp chopped Rosemary
1 clove garlic, finely chopped
1 heaped tsp sea salt
Freshly ground black pepper
Serves 4

Method
Pre-heat the oven to 160°C.
Score the skin of the belly pork
with a series of criss-cross
diagonal slashes. You will need
an extremely sharp knife, or an
artist's scalpel. Combine all the
dry marinade ingredients and
rub into the slashed surface of
the skin – as if you're giving a
massage! Chop all the
remaining vegetables and put in
the bottom of a roasting tin, big
enough to accommodate the
belly pork. Place the belly pork
on the veg and pour in the beer
and the tinned tomatoes. Add
the water until it comes about
2/3 of the way up the side of the
meat. Add the herbs and put in
the oven for about 4 hours.

Remove from the oven and
set aside to rest for no less
than fifteen minutes – this
allows the meat to relax and
the meat juices to flow into
the sauce giving added flavour.
After resting, remove the belly
and place on a chopping board.
With a sharp knife, carefully
cut the whole slab of meat
away from the ribs. Then pull
and cut away the crackling
and set aside for garnish. If
the crackling is not crispy
enough, just turn the oven up
to 200°C and put it back in the
oven for about ten minutes
(after separating it from the
meat). Carve the meat into
approximately 1 1/2 cm slices –
you'll need a really sharp knife,
but don't worry if the meat
falls apart a little – this is
all about flavour, not fancy
presentation. Serve up
the ribs as well – there's
stacks of juicy, succulent
meat between each
one just gagging to
be knawed off the
bone!

Beer glaze

Ingredients
300ml fruity ale
1 sprig thyme
1 sprig rosemary
1 tsp Dijon mustard
1 tsp honey
1 dsp Demerara sugar
40g butter
(Makes about 200ml of glaze)

Method
Put the beer, thyme and
rosemary into a pan and
reduce the liquid by half. Stir
in the rest of the ingredients,
strain to remove the herbs.
Use to brush meat for
barbecues or brush onto raw
vegetables before roasting.

PAR-COOKING TIP

COOK AS ABOVE, BUT ALLOW MEAT AND SAUCE
TO COOL BEFORE REFRIGERATING. TO SERVE,
SIMPLY HEAT SLICES OF BELLY PORK IN THE
OVEN, HEAT THE SAUCE AND SERVE WITH A
GOOD DOLLOP OF RE-HEATED MASH.

Dinner party

Beer glazed roast vegetables

This is one of the easiest complete vegetable dishes I know. While blanching requires each vegetable to be cooked independently – the roasting method allows all the veg to be thrown on the tray at the same time, and by some miraculous act of nature the whole lot is ready at the same time. This veggie medley will be as at home with a Sunday roast as it is with just a bowl of BBQ sauce for a light suppery snack.

Ingredients
1 head broccoli
2 courgettes
2 carrots
1 red onion
75ml beer glaze (see page 67)

A few sprigs of rosemary and thyme
2 or 3 bay leaves

Method
Divide the broccoli into small florets. Cut the courgettes on the bias into about 1 cm thick slices. Peel or wash the carrots and then cut lengthwise into 4 or six pieces per carrot depending on the size to make long spears. Peel the onion and cut into wedges. Spread the whole lot out on a baking tray and coat in the beer glaze. Add the herbs and season with sea salt and freshly ground black pepper. Put in a 180°C pre-heated oven for 35-45 minutes. The broccoli will get black and crispy around the edges, as will the tips of the carrots, but everything will still have a tender crunch and loads of roasted, beery flavour.

Rabbit and Leek Pie

Rabbit isn't one of those meats that leaps to mind when considering contemporary pie-fillings. Strange really, because historically, it's a pie classic. It returned to my cooking repertoire after a farm visit to the Lake District with a team from Loaded magazine. In a nutshell, there was lots of beer involved, and the day concluded with a rabbit stew cooked on an open fire by a babbling brook. Needless to say, it was a very good day.

Ingredients
600g boneless farmed rabbit
150g leek, trimmed and sliced
12 small shallots, peeled
150g button mushrooms
4 rashers streaky bacon, cut into a small dice (lardons)
100ml strong ale
250ml chicken stock
50g plain flour (seasoned with salt and pepper)
400g puff pastry
2 beaten eggs
2 tbsp chopped parsley
2 cloves garlic
(Serves 6, individual 150ml capacity pie dishes, or one large one)

Method
Cut the rabbit into cubes and coat in the seasoned flour. Pat off excess flour and reserve it for later. Heat a couple of tablespoons of olive oil in a heavy based saucepan and fry the rabbit pieces until lightly browned. Remove them from the pan and set aside. Fry the bacon lardons until lightly browned, remove and add to the rabbit. Add a little more oil to the saucepan and fry the onions until golden brown and tender. Repeat with the mushrooms and the leeks. Put all the meat and veg into the pan, add the remaining flour and cook out for a couple of minutes. Add the garlic and parsley and then pour over the beer and stock.

Bring to the boil and simmer for three to four minutes. Remove from the heat and allow to cool. Lightly flour a work surface and cut out the pastry lids by inverting the dish on the pastry and cutting around. Cut pastry strips to fit all around the rim of the pie dishes, Wet the rim and press on the pastry strips. Brush the pastry strips with egg wash and then fill the pie dishes with the rabbit mixture. Cover with the pastry lids, pinching all around to make a good seal. Brush the pastry lids with egg wash and prick with a fork to allow the steam to escape. Place in a 180°C pre-heated oven for 20-30 minutes, or until the pastry is golden brown and the filling is hot.

Dinner party

Glazed Chicken thighs

As far as chicken goes, I urge you to never settle for anything less than free range, and even then there are massive variations. Average free-range methods still involve processing more akin to intensive production. Try and source a local artisan producer such as Paul Talling's 'Loose Birds' from Harome in Yorkshire. Paul's birds are so free, easy and chilled-out, it's a wonder they don't fall out of their luxury penthouse coops. In fact, next to Paul's feathered friends, labelling free-range is like calling yourself an international playboy based on a couple of 18 to 30 holidays. The bottom line is: it's all reflected in the taste – a small extra price to pay for a such a taste experience.

Ingredients
8 chicken thighs

Marinade
200ml tomato juice
100ml pure orange juice
2 dsp runny honey
200ml full-flavoured beer
2 garlic cloves, finely sliced
A few sprigs of coriander
Serves 4

Method
Combine all the marinade ingredients together and marinate the chicken for at least two hours, preferably overnight. When ready to cook, remove the chicken pieces and dry them thoroughly on kitchen paper. Strain and reserve 200ml of the marinade. Heat a pan with a little oil and fry the chicken, skin side down, until it's golden brown and crispy. Turn it and add half the reserved marinade to the pan – do not pour over the skin, but rather, around the outside. Place in a 180°C, pre-heated oven for fifteen minutes. Remove the chicken from the pan, place in an oven proof serving dish and put back in the oven for a further ten to fifteen minutes. The chicken is cooked when the juices run clear when the thigh is pierced with a sharp knife. Pour the remaining reserved marinade into the frying pan with the other cooking liquor and stir well, scraping up any bits sticking to the bottom of the pan. Boil the liquid for several minutes to reduce the liquid to a syrupy consistency. Remove the chicken from the oven and pour the reduced marinade over it and serve.

Roast vegetable and taleggio cheese tart

This is a great dinner party starter, as it does away with the need to provide an alternative veggie option. Having said that, it actually makes a perfect veggie option – as the par-cooking method allows it to pretty much take care of itself for service – while you're at liberty to sort out everything else (such as pouring the drinks).

Ingredients

1 leek
1 courgette
1 aubergine
1 head broccoli
1 red pepper
2 red onions
Olive oil
Sea salt and pepper
A few sprigs of rosemary and/or thyme a few bay leaves
50g butter
125ml beer (Leffe Tripel)
375g packet ready rolled puff pastry
125g tomato pizza base topping
1 egg – beaten
Makes 6 tarts

Method

Cut the leek, courgette and aubergine on the bias into slices about 1cm thick. Break the broccoli in to small florets. Remove the skin from the onions and cut each one into 8 wedges. Cut the pepper in half, remove the stalk and seeds and cut into 6 pieces. Spread out the veg in one even layer on a baking tray and drizzle over the oil and season with sea salt and black pepper. Throw over the herbs. Roast in a 180°C pre-heated oven for about 30 minutes. Remove and pour over the beer and butter, boil the liquid on top of the stove for a couple of minutes making sure the vegetables are well coated with any liquid. Remove the skins from the peppers when cool enough to handle. To prepare the tarts, lightly flour a work surface and cut the pastry into six equal-sized squares. Spread the tomato sauce evenly over each one leaving a 1-2cm border all the way round. Divide the veg between each tart, piling it up on the tomato sauce. Brush the pastry borders with the egg wash and bake in a 180°C pre-heated oven for 10 minutes. Remove from the oven and top with slices of the cheese. Put back in the oven for a further 10 minutes. Serve with the roast tomato coulis and, if you wish, a good dollop of pesto.

PAR COOKING TIP

PREPARE THE VEGETABLES IN ADVANCE; COOL, COVER AND REFRIGERATE. JUST ASSEMBLE THE TARTS IN A MATTER OF MINUTES BEFORE YOU WANT TO BAKE THEM.

Dinner party

Cheesy beer fondue

This dish is so retro – it's downright cool again! Also, I love food for dinner parties that's shared and everyone just piles into it – it's just the ultimate catalyst for good communication. Clashing utensils, competing for the last morsel, or sitting back and offering it to a loved one are all part of the great dinner party experience. You can also use whatever you fancy to dip in the cheese: from cubes of cooked steak to crunchy raw vegetables. Just make sure you pile up more than you think you need – it will be eaten!

Ingredients
500g gruyère cheese (diced)
250ml wheat beer
1 tbsp potato flour
1 clove garlic
1 pinch ground nutmeg
1 whole brown loaf
salt and pepper to taste
Serves 6

Method
Rub the inside of the fondue pot or casserole dish with the cut clove of garlic, and leave in the pot for extra flavour. Pour in the beer and heat. Coat the cheese in the potato flour and add to the pot, whisking all the time while bringing slowly to a simmer. When all the cheese has melted, season with salt, pepper and nutmeg. Serve with the bread, cut into one-inch cubes.

Beer mash

You will find this one of the most versatile recipes in this book. It makes the filling for the BBQ'd sausage burger, and the baked sausages; it's the topping for pies as well as a great accompaniment to a whole bundle of dinner party dishes. It's also the ultimate stand-alone veg dish for the belly pork. Make sure you use a good quality floury potato such as Maris Piper. If you want an even richer version of this smooth velvety mash, just substitute a little of the milk with double cream – naughty, but nice!

Ingredients
600g Potatoes
60g butter
90ml milk
300ml beer – such as Old Speckled Hen
300ml water
Serves 4 as a main course accompaniament

Method
Peel the potatoes and cut into chunks. Place them in a pan and cover with the water, beer and good dsp of salt. If there isn't enough liquid to cover the potatoes, just add some more water until covered. Bring to the boil and simmer until the potatoes are just starting to break apart. Drain off the liquid, making sure that any residual moisture has evaporated. In the mean time, heat the milk and butter, being careful not to allow it to boil. Remove from the heat once the butter is melted. Mash the potato, ideally with a potato ricer, while it still warm. Immediately after the potato is mashed, fold in the warm butter and milk mixture. Add salt and white pepper to taste.

Smoked veggie chilli pie

This is one of those mate's mums recipes that you tend to accumulate when on the inevitable subject of food. The great thing about his one is its adaptability depending on time. For example, you don't have to put on the mash topping or stick it in the oven. It's a perfectly good veggie chilli as is. Just serve it up with some crusty bread or roast potato wedges, or even just a big bag of Tortillas.

Ingredients
200g green or brown lentils
150ml strong, full-flavoured beer (a strong English ale, Abbaye or Trappist beer)
2 onions, finely sliced
2 cloves garlic, crushed
2 tbsp olive oil
2 tbsp tomato purée
1 tsp smoked paprika
1/2 tsp chilli powder
1 tbsp Worcester Sauce
1 tin chopped tomatoes
1 tin kidney beans, drained
1 tin butter beans, drained

Mash
Serves 4

Method
Prepare the mash (see above). Put the lentils in a frying pan and pour over the beer – top up with water to cover. Bring to the boil and simmer for about 20 minutes – or until tender. Set aside. Cook the onions and garlic in the olive oil until soft, but without colour. Add the chilli powder and smoked paprika and cook for another couple of minutes. Add the tomato purée and cook, stirring regularly to avoid burning for two more minutes. Add the lentils plus all the remaining ingredients, except the potatoes and mix well. Put into an oven-proof dish and cover with the mash. Bake in a 180°C pre-heated oven for 30 minutes.

Dinner party

Ale Spring Chicken with creamed Savoy cabbage

Smooth hop character, full flavoured and creamy – and that's just the creamed cabbage accompaniment! This dish is beer heaven on a plate. The chicken is marinated in an oregano, sage and garlic with just a splash of a nutty brown ale such as Sam Smith's Organic, while the cabbage is simmered gently in cream and yet more ale. The beer adds depth and character to the dish without overpowering any element of it.

Ingredients
1 small chicken

For the marinade:
10g fresh sage
25g fresh oregano
1 clove garlic
Juice of 1 lemon
75ml beer
50ml olive oil
1 tsp honey
$1/2$ tsp salt
$1/2$ tsp black pepper

$1/2$ small Savoy cabbage
250ml double cream
Juice of half a lemon
50ml good British ale, such as Thwaites Lancaster Bomber
50g garden peas (cooked and refreshed)
Serves 2

Method
Blitz all the marinade ingredients together in a food processor. Remove the backbone from the chicken by turning it upside down and following the backbone down the length of the chicken with a sharp knife. Once loosened it can be easily cut out. Split the chicken in half by cutting through the breastbone lengthwise. Make three or four slits in the meat on each half, and pour over the marinade, rubbing it in all over, particularly into the incisions. Secure each chicken half with a wooden skewer, which has been soaked in water for at least an hour, to prevent burning. Marinade the chicken for at least two hours, preferably overnight.

To prepare the cabbage, finely slice and cook in the butter for 3-4 minutes. Add the cream and beer and simmer gently for about 15 minutes or until the cabbage is tender. This can then be left to cool. Add the peas and the lemon juice to the cooled cabbage.

To serve, cook the chicken in a pre-heated oven for about 25-40 minutes (it's cooked when the juices run clear when pierced with a knife in the thigh). While the chicken is resting, heat the cabbage. Arrange the cabbage in the centre of the plate and place the chicken resting up against it.

Honey and lemon braised fennel

One of my all time favourite veggie dishes – it's so good you could serve it as a veggie main course with nothing but a chilled glass of lemony wheat beer! It could also be easily adapted for the BBQ just by re-heating over coals and serving the sauce separately or poured over the fennel once it's in a serving dish.

Ingredients
4 Fennel bulbs
160g butter
Juice of 4 lemons
4 tsp runny honey
4ooml chicken stock
(a stock cube is fine)
400ml wheat beer
200ml double cream
40g fresh grated Parmesan

Method
Cut each fennel bulb in half, and then cut each half into 3 wedges – or 4 if the fennel is particularly large. Gently heat the butter in a pan – large enough to fit all the fennel in a single layer. Cook in 2 pans if you can't do this. Place the fennel, flat side down, and cook gently until they start to brown. Turn and repeat on the other flat side, finishing with them resting on their rounded side. Brown on this side too, and then pour over the stock, beer, lemon and honey. Cook very gently for about 20 minutes – or until the fennel is just tender. Remove the fennel and set aside. Strain the cooking liquor, return to the pan and reduce by half. Add the cream and reduce to about 200ml (about $3/4$) the sauce should be quite thick. Remove from the heat. Place the fennel in an ovenproof dish. Pour over the sauce and sprinkle with grated Parmesan. Bake in a 180°C oven for 15 minutes. Serve.

Dinner party

Method
Soak the sultanas in the beer overnight. When you're ready to cook, pre-heat the oven to180°C. Peel and quarter the apples, remove the cores and cut each quarter into about 6 chunks. Melt the 50g of butter, drain the sultanas and then add all the ingredients and cook gently for about 20 minutes, or until the apple is soft, but still retains its shape. Remove from the heat and allow to stand for 30 minutes. To prepare the filo, take a 17cm x 28cm sheet and lay on a work surface with the long edge running horizontally. Brush the whole sheet with melted butter, lay another sheet on top of the first and brush again with melted butter. Repeat one more time making a total of three, buttered layers. Spread a quarter of the mixture evenly along the the pastry leaving a border of about 6cm at ech end and 5cm top and bottom. Fold the ends of the pastry in towards the middle. Then, fold the bottom edge up and over and then roll creating a spring roll-like cylinder. Brush with more melted butter, and place on a baking tray lined with kitchen parchment paper. Cook the filos in the oven for about 25 minutes – or until the pastry is golden brown. Just beware of hot filling if you can't wait to bite into it!

Beer poached pears

Beer is an ideal liquid for poaching fruit – it's got so much more flavour than a wine and water combo! A good dose of sugar or honey will balance out any inherent bitterness, while the fruit, herbal and spicy elements of quality speciality beers are perfect matches for the juicy pear.

Ingredients
4 pears
750ml caster sugar
350ml water
350ml wheat beer
1 cinnamon stick
3 slices lemon
1 star anise
3 cloves
Serves 4

Method
Bring the sugar, beer and water to the boil. Turn down the heat and add all the other ingredients except the pears. Simmer for 20 minutes and allow to cool. Peel the pears, halve and remove the cores. Place the pears in the cooled poaching liquid and bring to the boil. Remove from the heat and allow the pears to cool in the syrup.

Apple, cinnamon and sultana filo

Ingredients
600g cooking apples
50g butter
150g demerara sugar
150g sultanas
100 ml English strong ale such as Fullers 1845
2 tsp ground cinnamon
200g filo pastry
100g butter, melted
Serves 4

Hoegaarden and lychee semi-freddo

This classic Italian dessert translates as 'half cold'. It's similar to ice cream, but you don't need an ice cream maker, or have the aggravation of churning it every few minutes. The refreshing zestiness of a wheat beer is a wonderful foil for the sweetness of the lychees. You also have a choice of presentation – either make it in a terrine mould and then slice into slabs for service, or simply pour into ramekins, set and serve.

Ingredients
4 egg yolks
75g caster sugar
425g tin of lychees
45g icing sugar
250ml double cream
2 egg whites
100ml wheat beer
Makes 8 ramekins

Method
Lightly beat the egg yolks and caster sugar until they are smooth and pale. Drain the lychees and purée with the beer and icing sugar in a food processor. Whip the cream until it thickens to the point where it just holds its form; whisk the egg whites until they form soft peaks. Mix all the ingredients together, gently folding in the whisked egg whites. Pour into the ramekins and leave to set in the freezer for at least 4-5 hours.

When it comes to sexy, smoochy, luv-inducing potions – beer is perhaps not the beverage that leaps to the front of the mind. But before you dismiss this chapter as pure beer-goggled fantasy, please hear me out.

Imagine this beverage scenario: A naturally spritzy, lightly fruity, slightly tangy, burnished red, champagne flute of beer. This is beer of the sexiest kind: The Lambic fruit beers of Belgium are made for romance. They don't have any of the bitterness normally associated with beer. I've taken cases of these beers to dinner parties and had the female contingent literally begging for more!

Having sampled your soft, fruity side, your partner will be ready for a bit of smooth, dark and silky action – how about a single oyster, coated in a light tempura batter sat on a shot glass of dark, creamy stout. There's not a pint pot in sight – just a tempting, lip-smacking snifter to stimulate the appetite. Moving swiftly, but seductively on, and it's a case of herbal heaven meets light, fresh fish, when a wine-sized glass of zesty wheat beer is the perfect partner for all manner of seafood dishes. Just make sure that dishes aren't too hefty – keep it coming, but in small quantities – we're trying to induce fun and frivolity here – not lethargy or sleep.

So you get my drift? From a male recipient's point of view: how thoughtful to be provided with the beverage so close to our hearts? From the female perspective: how daringly different and adventurous.

Romance & adventure

Asparagus with wheat beer Hollandaise

Make no mistake, Asparagus is sexy, particularly the English stuff which has an incredibly short six-week season between mid-May and the end of June. Dipped in melted butter, or with a luscious Hollandaise, the slender spears should be fed, by fingers, to waiting partner's mouth!

Ingredients
400g Asparagus
2 tbsp Hollandaise sauce
(see page 24)

Method
Bend the Asparagus so it breaks according to its natural breaking point – you can then trim the ends to make them even. Bring a large pan of salted water to the boil, and add the Asparagus. After a couple of minutes, test for doneness by removing a stalk and tasting. It should be giving, but still retain a certain bite (al dente). As soon as it is cooked; drain and refresh under cold running water until cool. Drain and refrigerate until required. To serve, heat a knob of butter with a tablespoon of water. When the water starts to bubble and the butter has melted, add the asparagus and toss gently with some sea salt and freshly ground black pepper.

PAR-COOKING TIP

THE BLANCHING IN BOILING WATER AND REFRESHING UNDER COLD WATER IS A STANDARD PAR-COOKING PROCESS FOR MOST VEGETABLES THAT ARE TO BE HEATED AND SERVED LATER. THE INITIAL COOKING SHOULD LEAVE THEM A FRACTION ON THE UNDER-DONE SIDE, AS THE FINAL BLAST OF HEAT WILL BRING THEM TO PERFECTION.

Raspberry beer crème fraîche dressing

A salad dressing may not be the recipe that leaps to the front of your mind when trying to list a top twenty sexy foodstuffs. All that oil – fine if it doesn't remind you of olives or chips – and then vinegar? – Big turn off. So, a little substitution is required to transform this salady stalwart into something more seductive. Trust the French to come up with the very ingredient: their version of double cream is crème fraîche – smooth as satin, slightly piquant and very creamy. A little raspberry beer reduction and you've got a ready-made addition to all manner of juicy little starters and salads. You can do the same thing with any of the lambic fruit beers. These beers are not bitter, so there's no problem reducing them, unlike hoppy beers which will really concentrate the bitterness when you boil off the water.

Ingredients
1 x 375ml bottle raspberry beer
Crème fraîche

Method
Pour the beer into a saucepan and place over a medium heat, skim off any foam that forms on top. Reduce to 50ml. Allow to cool and then stir into the crème fraîche.

Seared scallops with beer beurre blanc and samphire

Samphire is a delicious, seasonal, marsh-dwelling vegetable, sometimes referred to as sea asparagus. The season begins in early July and runs throughout summer. Your local fishmonger – if you're lucky enough to have one – should stock it. If you can't get hold of any, substitute it for any other green vegetable such as spinach, fine green beans, or even a simple pile of salad leaves. The quantities here are for a starter portion, so just double up for a very sexy main course.

Ingredients
6 King Scallops
30g shallots, finely chopped
Juice of 1 lemon
150ml Wheat beer
125g butter
50ml cream
Pinch of salt
Handful of samphire

Method
To make the beurre blanc: Put the shallots, lemon juice and wheat beer in a saucepan, bring to the boil and then continue to simmer until you're left with about a dessertspoon of liquid. Remove from the heat. Cut the cold butter into small cubes and then put the saucepan with the reduction over a low heat. Start to add the butter, a couple of cubes at a time, into the saucepan with the reduction, agitating the pan all the time allowing the butter to blend smoothly. It should maintain a coating consistency and be smooth and pale yellow. Don't be tempted to turn the heat up to accelerate the process as this may split the sauce. Only add the next batch of butter when the preceding one has become fully amalgamated. Once you have used up all the butter, and have a smooth sauce, you can add the cream. This helps stabilise the beurre blanc and stops it splitting if you re-heat it later. Strain the sauce into a clean pan through a fine sieve, leaving behind the shallot residue.

Meanwhile, bring a pan of water to the boil and add the samphire. Boil for about a minute and then drain. Prepare the scallops by removing the white, gristly nodule on the edge of the scallop with a sharp knife. Leaving the orange coral intact is a matter of personal preference. Heat a frying pan until very hot, season the scallops with salt and freshly ground pepper, add a dessertspoon of oil to the pan and fry the scallops for a couple of minutes on each side, turning only when they have a nice golden brown caramelised surface. The scallop should be opaque in the middle i.e. slightly under-cooked. To serve, heap a pile of samphire in the middle of the plate, pour the sauce around the sapphire and then arrange the scallops around the plate.

PAR-COOKING TIP

PREPARE THE BEURRE BLANC AS ABOVE AND SET ASIDE. BLANCHE THE SAMPHIRE AS ABOVE AND THEN IMMEDIATELY REFRESH UNDER COLD RUNNING WATER, DRAIN AND SET ASIDE. WHEN YOU'RE READY TO SERVE, JUST TOSS THE SAMPHIRE IN A FRYING PAN WITH A KNOB OF BUTTER AND A DESSERTSPOON OF WATER UNTIL HEATED THROUGH, AND WARM THE BEURRE BLANC. ALL THIS CAN BE DONE IN THE TIME IT TAKES TO PAN-FRY THE SCALLOPS.

Romance & adventure

Warm duck breast and artichoke salad

Salads are perfect dishes for romantic dinners. For one, the prep is minimal, thus eliminating the risk of beginning the meal looking as though you've just gone head to head over 110m with Colin Jackson on a particularly hot day. Secondly, they are light: I don't know about you, but after the merest morsel of heavy food in the evening, I'm subject to bouts of uncontrollable narcolepsy – not good for the art of seduction. A raspberry beer is a natural choice with the duck, and obviously matches up with the dressing. However, a French bière de garde or a Saison beer from southern Belgium would also make a spritzy, sexy accompaniment.

Ingredients
1 or 2 duck breasts, depending on size
4 tinned artichoke hearts, cut in quarters
2 handfuls mixed salad (spinach, rocket, watercress)
2 dsp raspberry beer crème fraîche dressing (see page 81)
1 dozen raspberries

Method
Pre-heat the oven to 180°C. Trim any excess fat from around the edge of the duck breast and then score the skin with a series of diagonal lines about 1cm apart. Repeat in the opposite direction creating a lattice appearance. Use a sharp knife and be careful just to pierce the fat, not the meat. Heat an empty frying pan on a medium to high heat, season the skin side with salt and pepper and put skin side down in the frying pan. Don't worry about putting it in a dry pan – it will render enough fat to fry itself in. Season the other side and turn when the skin is golden brown. Add the artichoke quarters to the same pan and place in the oven for about 7 minutes (for medium rare). Remove and allow to rest for 5 minutes. Slice the duck on the bias into thin slices. Put the salad and raspberries in a mixing bowl, add the duck, artichoke and and 3 dsps of raspberry beer crème fraîche dressing. Toss gently and divide equally between two plates.

Tempura oysters with a stout shot

I remember serving this one as a canapé at a very exclusive private bash many years ago. It was during my apprenticeship days with one of London's best private dining chefs, Colin Easby, and it's stuck in my memory ever since – I really can't think of a sexier way to serve up this classic combo.

Ingredients

For the batter
1 egg
25ml fridge-cold stout
or porter
50ml iced water
70g sifted flour

12 Live oysters
Serves 2

Method

To make the batter, gently beat the eggs and add the stout and water, lightly beating with a fork. Add the sifted flour, and very gently, amalgamate the mixture, making sure you KEEP the mixture lumpy. Shuck the oysters with an oyster knife and drain off the liquid. Ideally you should use a thermostat controlled deep fat fryer between 175° and 195°C. Failing this, heat a pan of oil to this temperature. This is dangerous and you should keep a constant eye on it. Make sure the oil doesn't come more than 3/4 of the way up to the pan. It is up to temperature when a cube of fresh bread browns in 1 minute. Dip the oysters into the batter and very carefully lower them into the hot oil. They will be ready in approximately 1 minute. Remove with a slotted spoon and drain on kitchen paper. Serve with one on top of a shot glass of Porter or stout of your choice.

Romance & adventure

Monkfish, haddock and saffron fish cakes

Ingredients
150g new potatoes
Big pinch of saffron
100g Monkfish
100g Haddock fillet
10 large basil leaves,
finely sliced
1 ¹/₂ dsp mayonnaise
(see page 87)
¹/₂ tsp salt
2 dsp olive oil
20g polenta

Method
Cut the potatoes into small, evenly sized pieces, place in a pan and just cover with cold water. Add the saffron and a good pinch of salt. Bring to the boil and simmer until the potatoes are cooked through. Drain, crush lightly with a fork and reserve. In the meantime, chop up the Monkfish and Haddock into approximately ¹/₂ cm pieces. Combine in a bowl the reserved crushed potato, mayonnaise, basil and seasoning. Shape the mixture into patties and then coat in the polenta, patting off any excess. Heat the oil in a frying pan and fry the fish cakes for a few minutes on each side until golden brown, and then transfer to a 180ºC pre-heated oven for fifteen minutes. Serve with a fragrant, zesty wheat beer such a Erdinger or Hoegaarden, or a good floral pilsner like Urquell, Budvar or Staropramen.

Gruyère and stout tart

This is another of those stress-free, no-sweat dishes when it comes to service. The tarts can be made up to 2 or 3 days in advance and then simply banged through the oven for fifteen minutes or so, to heat through. You can then dress the dish up any which way you want. Personally, a few mixed leaves perched on top of the tart with a little basil, or other flavoured oil does it for me. A few oven roast tomatoes scattered around the edge can give an extra flash of colour to lift the presentation. As far as the beer accompaniment goes, I would favour a toffee-ish, English ale such as Old Speckled Hen. Its caramel sweetness matches perfectly with the onions, while the mellow hop flavour is a natural choice with the cheese.

Ingredients
150g short crust pastry
1/2 onion, finely sliced
10g butter
2 dsp veg oil
50ml porter or stout
50g Gruyère cheese, finely grated
2 eggs
150ml double cream
2 spring onions, finely chopped
1/2 tsp salt
Freshly ground black pepper
Serves 2

Method
Pre heat the oven to 180°C. In a frying pan melt the butter with the oil and add the finely sliced onion. Cook gently until very soft and deep golden brown. Add the porter and bubble on the heat for a further 10-15 seconds. Remove from the heat and set aside to cool. Combine the egg, cream, grated Gruyère, spring onion, salt and a few grinds of the pepper mill. When the onion/beer mixture has cooled, add that too. Butter two pie dishes of about 12cm diameter and 4 cm deep, and line with the thinly rolled out pastry. Blind bake for 10 mins filled with some dried beans wrapped in a cling film parcel. Remove the cling film parcel and return to the oven for another five minutes. Stir the filling well and pour evenly between the two pastry dishes. Turn the oven up to 190°C and bake for 15-20 minutes, or until the top is golden brown and just set. Remove from the oven and allow to cool, before refrigerating. To serve, just heat through in a 180°C pre-heated oven for about fifteen minutes.

MAYO TIP
IF THE MAYO SPLITS, JUST WHISK IN A FEW DROPS OF LUKE WARM WATER, AND THINGS SHOULD COME BACK TOGETHER.

Wheat Beer Mayonnaise

Ingredients
1 large egg yolk
2 tsp wheat beer
2 tsp lemon juice
1 tsp Dijon mustard
200ml vegetable oil
Salt and freshly ground white pepper

Method
Combine the egg yolk, mustard, beer and lemon juice in a bowl and gradually whisk in the oil – a few drops at a time at first, and then in a slow, steady stream. Season to taste with salt and freshly ground white pepper.

Romance & adventure

Salmon Niçoise Salad

Ingredients
200g poached salmon
(see page 26)
100g fine beans
170g new potatoes
12 quails' eggs
2 handfuls of mixed leaves
(spinach, watercress and rocket)
small handful pitted black
olives

For the dressing
2 dsp crème fraîche
1 tsp lemon juice
1 dsp olive oil

Method
Poach the salmon according to the scrambled eggs and salmon recipe on page 26. Allow to cool. Bring a large pan of salted water to the boil. Top and tail the beans and put into the boiling water for about 3 minutes, or until just cooked with a light crunch. Remove the beans with a slotted spoon and plunge immediately into cold water. Keep cold water running over the beans until cool. Slice the new potatoes into 1cm pieces and put into the boiling bean water. Cook for a few minutes until just cooked with a little bite. Remove and cool in the same way as the beans, under cold running water. Add the quails' eggs to the boiling water and boil for exactly 2$^{1}/_{2}$ mins. Cool once again under cold running water. Peel the eggs by lightly cracking all over. Pinch the shell at the bottom and peel away the shell finishing at the top of the egg. Rinse off any tiny bits of residual shell and set aside. To serve, combine all the ingredients in a large bowl, flaking in the salmon. Combine the dressing ingredients and drizzle over the salad.

Romance & adventure

Deep fried Roquefort

This is a recipe I've adapted from the one I used to prepare when I was a chef de partie at Blakes in London – undoubtedly, one of the world's sexiest hotels. Molten cheese, oozing out of wafer thin crispy filo, spreading seductively over those piled up leaves... ooh err, I should say so!

Ingredients
200g Roquefort cheese
60g cream cheese
Packet of filo pastry
75g butter
150g mixed leaf salad

2 dsp of raspberry beer crème fraîche (see recipe on page 81)
Serves 2

Method
Take 100g of the Roquefort, and mix with the cream cheese. This is easier if the cheeses have been sat at room temperature for a while to soften-up. Also, using a food processor helps to get a smoother mix. Add the chives and from into 4 equal size balls. Melt the butter. Lay a sheet of filo on a chopping board and cut into a 16cm square. Brush with the butter. Lay another sheet of filo on top of the first, cut to the same size as the first one and brush with butter. Place a ball of cheese in the middle of the filo. Gather up the corners; bring together and twist, forming a ball shape parcel. You will have a dramatic looking fan of filo rising up from the top of the ball which crisps up beautifully when deep fried. Be careful not to tear the filo as you twist. Repeat the process for the other 3 balls. When ready to serve, deep fry the filo parcels at about 180°C until golden brown and drain on kitchen paper.

Deep fry the parcels until they're golden brown. Crumble the remaining Roquefort into the salad and spoon over the dressing, with the raspberriess. Arrange the salad on two plates with the deep fried filo parcels and serve.

HOT TIP!

IF YOU DON'T HAVE A DEEP FAT FRYER, BRING A LARGE PAN OF VEGETABLE OIL UP TO ABOUT 175°C. IT HAS REACHED THIS TEMPERATURE WHEN A CUBE OF FRESH BREAD WILL BROWN IN ABOUT 1 MINUTE.

 BE EXTREMELY CAREFUL, AS THE OIL WILL EVENTUALLY CATCH FIRE IF IT GETS TOO HOT.

Strawberry crème brûlée

Ingredients
200g strawberries
200ml Fruli strawberry beer
2 dsp caster sugar
1/2 pint double cream
3 egg yolks
1/2 a vanilla pod

Method
Remove the cores from all the strawberries and cut them into thin slices. Heat the beer until simmering, scrape off any foam, remove from the heat and add the sliced strawberries. Set aside to cool down. Divide the strawberry mixture between the two ramekins and chill in the freezer. To make the brûlée, pour the cream into heavy based saucepan, split the vanilla pod along it's length and scrape the seeds out into the cream and add the pod. Heat until just before it boils and remove from the heat. Whisk the egg yolks and sugar for a minute or two, until smooth, Strain the cream onto the egg and sugar mixture through a fine sieve. Return to a clean, heavy based saucepan and stir over a low heat for about 8 minutes – or until the mixture thickens and becomes slightly gelatinous. Do not allow it to boil. Remove from the heat. Take the ramekins from the freezer and pour over the brûlée mixture and put in the fridge to set overnight.

Romance & adventure

Strawberry jelly petits fours

If this little palate cleanser – casually delivered at the end of the meal – doesn't get you everything you're dreaming of from a romantic night in, then nothing will. It's about as sexy as food ever gets while still being food! On this occasion I have no qualms about breaking my golden rule about utilising seasonal produce – if English strawberries are in season, make sure you get them. If not, who gives a damn – this is far more important than food!

Ingredients
250ml strawberry beer
45g sugar
3 leaves of gelatine
8 strawberries
Makes 8 little jellies

Method
Line a rectangular tray or mould (about 8cm x 4cm x 2cm deep) with a double layer of cling film, making sure the cling film overlaps the lip of the mould. Cut each strawberry across the diameter, discarding the end with the leaf. You want to be left with a strawberry section about $^1/_2$ cm tall. To make the jelly; heat the beer and sugar until the sugar dissolves. Skim off any surface foam and remove from the heat. While the sugar is dissolving, submerge the gelatine leaves in cold water for several minutes until they soften. Squeeze them out and add to the warm liquid – stirring until the gelatine has completely dissolved. Pour $^1/_3$ of the liquid jelly into the mould to about $^1/_2$ cm deep. Put in the fridge. Once set (about $^1/_2$ an hour, remove

from fridge and place the strawberries, flat-side-down, on the jelly, spacing evenly. Pour another layer of liquid jelly to come about $^1/_2$ way up the strawberry (not so much liquid to float the strawberries). Return to the fridge. Once set, repeat the process a final time with the remaining liquid jelly – submerging the strawberries. They should now appear to be suspended in the jelly. Return to the fridge. To serve: carefully lift the jelly out of the mould by the cling film, and place on a chopping board. Dip a sharp knife in hot water and cut the jelly into even-size squares. Admire and serve!

Fruli chocolate tart

Ingredients
For the pastry
250g plain flour
125g unsalted butter (diced and softened)
70g caster sugar
$^1/_2$ large beaten egg

For the filling
250g chocolate
125g unsalted butter
100ml fruity beer, such as Adnams Broadside
3 egg yolks
2 whole eggs
50g caster sugar
Makes a tart 16cm x 2.5cm (a flan tin of about these dimensions is required)

Method
First, make the pastry: if you have a food processor, just whiz all the pastry ingredients for a few seconds – until they form into a ball. If you don't have one, sieve the flour into a bowl, and work in the butter and sugar with your fingertips. Make a well in the middle and add the beaten egg. Knead the mixture with your fingers, wrap in cling film, and rest in the fridge for about thirty minutes. Lightly flour a work surface and roll out the pastry as thin as possible. Lightly butter the flan tin and lay the pastry inside, leaving an overhang (you trim this off later). Cut a circle of greaseproof paper to fit inside, and up the sides of the flan tin, place on the pastry and cover with dried beans to blind bake. Place in a 180°C pre-heated oven for about ten minutes. Remove the beans and greaseproof paper and put back in the oven for another ten minutes.

While the pastry is baking, make the filling. Break up the chocolate, and put in a bowl with the butter and beer, and set over a pan of simmering water. When melted, remove from the heat and stir until smooth. Whisk the eggs, egg yolks and sugar until smooth, and pour in the chocolate mixture, stirring until fully amalgamated. Pour into the pastry case, turn the oven up to 220°C, and bake for five minutes. Allow to cool and refrigerate overnight.

Food for sport

One of the most pleasurable aspects of watching sport on TV is the consumption of food and beer that seems to naturally accompany it. I think it's the juxtaposition of the on-screen exertions and the sloth-like couch life that gives the whole process of consumption an added decadence – a kind of naughty-but-nice vibe. Throw in a major cup final, play-off, grand slam, or any big sporting scenario that rocks your boat and you're dealing with a potential festival on the scale of Mardi Gras. It's only right then, that the eating experience matches the sporting one – but with a few rules thrown in to make for an entertaining and clean game. Firstly, crockery should be kept to a minimum, and ideally, cutlery done away with altogether.

Double top for a famous victory!

No fork required!

In 1608, the writer, Thomas Coryat, returned to England after travels in Europe, and began eating with a fork he'd acquired in Venice. His use of an implement to transport food from plate to mouth was greeted with incredulity, and in true British style, the mick was well and truly taken. You see we are, and have always been, a sports-loving nation; which means we spend a great deal of time standing up – particularly in the days before television when the mountain could not be brought to Muhammad. Clearly, under such circumstances, with beer in hand, an eating implement is a useless encumbrance. It's worth remembering then, how the fork-bearing scribe was received when we consider what food to serve at our sporting gatherings.

Whatever it is you eventually come up with, there is one, key proviso. Regardless of how long initial prep took you, the actual heating and serving should take no longer than the allotted fifteen minutes of half-time.

A little pre-match prep

Food for sport

NICK Cheers mate!

Smoked chunky chilli

My mate Nick makes the finest chilli I have ever eaten – by a street. This is his recipe – cheers Nick! My addition is simply the beer, which has the two-fold effect of being a marinade for the chunks of beef, but also gives a further depth of flavour through its addition to the chilli itself. While a full- flavoured strong beer is most suited to the actual cooking, I would tend to have a good pilsner such as Urquell, or a Mexican beer like Dos Equis, as an accompaniment – they'll be more refreshing, and perform that important 'cut and cleanse' routine.

Ingredients
300g braising steak
100ml strong, full-flavoured beer
500g minced beef
30g red chillies, finely chopped
1 onion, finely chopped
2 cloves garlic, crushed
1/2 tsp hot chilli powder
1 tsp smoked paprika
1 dsp tomato purée
1 tin chopped tomatoes
1 tin kidney beans, drained of liquid
Salt and pepper
Makes 6 x good sized bowls

Method
Cut the braising steak into small cubes, approx 1cm square. Pour the beer over the steak and leave overnight in the fridge. To make the chilli, drain the marinated beef, reserving the marinating liquid and pat the meat dry on kitchen paper. Fry the meat until it browns, remove from the pan and set aside. Brown the mince in the same pan, and set aside, with the braising steak including any meat juices. Fry the onions, garlic and chopped chilli for a few minutes until they start to soften. Add the chilli powder and paprika and carry on frying for a couple more minutes. Keep stirring so the mixture doesn't burn on the bottom of the pan. Add the tomato purée and fry for a couple more minutes, while stirring. Put the meat back in the pan along with the tinned tomatoes and the reserved marinating liquor, and simmer very gently for at least an hour and a half. Fifteen minutes before the end of cooking, add the drained kidney beans.

Handful of grated cheddar
12 dsp soured cream
Makes 12 Tacos

Method

First make the tomato salsa:
Cut the tomatoes into quarters,
remove the seeds, along with
the excess juice and set aside.
Cut the flesh into a small dice,
and then chop up the core and
add back to the chopped flesh
along with any juice. Finely
dice the red onion and add to
the tomato. De-seed and finely
chop the chillies and add to
the mix along with the finely
chopped coriander. Season
with salt and pepper to taste,
and store in the fridge until
required.

Next, make the avocado and
cucumber salad: Peel the
cucumber and scrape out the
seeds. Cut into thin strips
lengthwise and then cut across
to get a small dice. Peel the
avocado, remove the stone,
and cut into a similar size dice
to the cucumber and add to it.
Add the lime juice, chopped
coriander, salt and pepper and
mix well. Refrigerate until it's
required.

To serve, heat the Taco shells
according to the instructions on
the packet and heat the chilli
either on the stove, or in the
microwave. Spread a spoonful
of the avocado salad in the
bottom of each Taco, spoon
chilli over the top and sprinkle
over some grated cheddar,
spoon over a little more
avocado mix. Top with tomato
salsa and soured cream.

**Chilli Tacos with avocado and cucumber salad
and tomato salsa**

This is the ultimate Mexican – munchie combo:
all colour and full-on flavour. Just make sure you
supply stacks of paper towels! You could do a
Nacho version if you wished – just pile high with
layers of Nachos, chilli and cheese, bung the whole
lot in the oven until melting and hot, before
garnishing with all the accompaniments.

Ingredients
**Smoked chunky chillli
(see page 96)
12 Taco shells
2 avocados
1/2 cucumber
1 tsp lime juice
2 dsp chopped coriander
Salt and pepper**

**For the tomato salsa
6 fresh plum tomatoes
1/2 red onion
3 dsp chopped coriander
30g red chillies
Salt and pepper**

Food for sport

Inside-out hot dogs with BBQ sauce dip

When I worked on the London event catering / canapé party scene, a miniaturized version of this – using tiny cocktail sausages – was all the rage at the trendiest launch parties and premiers. Waitresses used to have to use all kinds of escape and evasion techniques if they were ever to get from one end of the room to the other before their entire trays were devoured. Obviously, you could do the same single-bite versions for yourselves for the right occasion. However, I think food for sport needs something a little less twee. As far as beer goes, I can't really think of one that doesn't go with sausages!

Ingredients
10 quality sausages of your choice
6oz Beer mash (see page 73)
Bowl of BBQ sauce (see page 52)

Method
Make the mash according to the recipe on page 73 Cook the sausages in a 200°C pre-heated oven until brown and cooked through (about 25 minutes). When cool enough to handle, slit the sausages lengthwise down the middle, not quite cutting all the way through. Put the mash in a piping-bag and pipe into the middle of the sausage. If you don't have a piping-bag, you can make one with a sheet of kitchen parchment paper: just fold in half and then make a conical funnel by bringing the top right corner down to the bottom left, Cut off at the end to make a hole large enough for the mash to squeeze through, and secure the paper by turning down the 'v' at the top to form an even round opening. Fill with mash and pipe away.

PAR-COOKING TIP

COOK THE SAUSAGES AND ALLOW TO COOL. DO THE SAME WITH THE MASH. WHEN COOL, PIPE THE MASH INTO THE SAUSAGES, COVER AND REFRIGERATE UNTIL REQUIRED. TO SERVE, SIMPLY HEAT THROUGH IN A 180°C PRE-HEATED OVEN FOR 10-15 MINUTES.

Food, sport, beer and mates – it doesn't get any better!

Cheese and Ham Bread

This is a mouth-watering classic combo of ham, cheese, bread and beer. It applies the same slicing, stuffing and baking principles as garlic bread, but with a meatier punch. Any full flavoured, malty, hoppy ale is ideal for this. Just make sure you make enough!

Ingredients
4 small baguettes
250g/8oz grated Gruyère cheese
Milk
Beer
45g butter
45g plain flour
200g lardons (pancetta cut into small cubes)
400ml beer
Makes 4 small baguettes

Method
Fry the pancetta in a dessert spoon of oil until golden brown, drain onto kitchen paper and set aside. Next, make the cheese sauce: Heat the milk in a pan until just simmering. While the milk is heating, melt the butter in a separate pan and add the flour. Cook for a few minutes stirring regularly. The flour and butter mixture (the roux) is ready when it's sandy in texture, but not coloured. At this point, remove it from the heat and allow to cool. When the roux is cool, add the hot milk, a little at a time, whisking or stirring constantly until smooth. Add the cheese and stir until smooth again. Remove it from the heat, add the reserved lardons and cool in the fridge until the sauce has solidified.

Slice the baguette at a slight angle at about 2cm intervals, taking care not to slice it all the way through. Fill the gaps with the cheesy filling and then wrap the whole baguette in kitchen foil. Bake in a 180°C pre-heated oven for about 20-25 minutes. Unwrap and serve.

Food for sport

Roast paprika potato wedges

There's obviously no reason why you can't serve this as a potato accompaniment to any main course dish you fancy. But as finger footie-food, they don't half make a great gastro alternative to a bag of crisps. As far as dips go – anything goes. Personally, I like a good mayonnaise – I guess it's that late night Amsterdam chips and mayo thing that's never quite left me – try the wheat beer mayo on page 87.

Ingredients
1kg maris piper potatoes, or similar
500ml full-flavoured ale, such as Fullers ESB
500ml water
1 dsp salt
120g butter
1 dsp sweet smoked paprika

Method
Wash the potatoes, then cut into wedges by cutting in half lengthwise – keep the skins on. Cut each half into 3 or 4 wedges depending on potato size. Put in a pan with the water, beer and salt, and bring to the boil. Simmer for 10-14 minutes, or until just beginning to go a little soft, but not near breaking up. Drain well, and put back on the stove for 30 seconds or so to get rid of any residual moisture. When they're cool enough to handle, scrape a fork down each flat edge of each wedge. This 'roughing-up' is optional, depending on how much time you've got, but it really helps get a lovely, crispy finish. Arrange the wedges in a single layer in a baking tin, sprinkle with the paprika and dot with knobs of butter. Roast in the top of a 200°C pre-heated oven for 20 mins to half an hour, or until golden brown and crispy on the outside.

PAR-COOKING TIP

COOK AS ABOVE, THEN ALLOW TO COOL AND SIMPLY RE-HEAT AND CRISP-UP IN A 180°C PRE-HEATED OVEN FOR ABOUT 15 MINUTES.

Welsh rarebit

This is the original beer and food combo,
and is perhaps even more famous than the
ubiquitous steak and ale pie. It's actually
one of my all time favourite snacks – it's as
appropriate as a midnight munchie as it is for
a lazy Sunday breakfast, and you can throw in all
kinds of add-ons depending on occasion, mood, or
fridge stock: eggs of any variety, bacon, mixed salad and balsamic
dressing, or all of the above in one glorious pile. For instant, future gratification,
prepare the rarebit as above, up until before the grilling stage. You can then
freeze the whole slices, separating them with sheets of kitchen parchment
paper. When a rarebit attack strikes you, simply take a frozen slice and whack
it straight under a hot grill, it will defrost and melt the cheese in one go.

Ingredients
**250g mature grated
cheddar**
**100ml wheat beer, such as
O'Hanlon's Double Champion**
1 tsp English mustard powder
1 egg yolk
**A few drops of Worcester
sauce**
4 slices of bread
Makes 4 slices of rarebit

Method
Mix all the ingredients together
in a bowl, or ideally, blitz in a
food processor to a paste. Toast
the bread on both sides and
then spread the mixture in a
thick layer on the toast making
sure you cover the crusts too.
Put under a hot grill until it
goes golden brown and serve
immediately

Food for sport

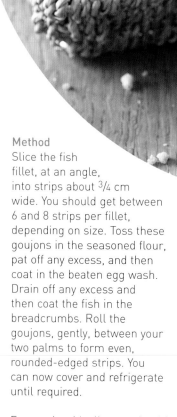

Fish and Chip Cones with tartare sauce

Combine the nation's favourite meal, with an easily held vessel and bite-size pieces of fish, and you're backing a sure-fire winner – regardless of what the betting slip says. Believe me, this one will go a long way making up for a lost match or lost money. If you really want to go to town, create a bespoke cone design on your computer and print them out– endless possibilities for commemorative laughs! As far as beer goes, the same zesty wheat beer you've used for the tartare sauce would be delicious. A chilled pilsner would refresh and cut through any residual oiliness, while a malty ale will compare favourably with vinegar and will still not overpower the lightness of the fish.

Ingredients
700g plaice or lemon sole fillet, skinned
60g breadcrumbs
2 eggs, beaten
4 tbsp plain flour, seasoned with salt and pepper

2 handfuls of chips
Tartare sauce
6 tbsp mayonnaise
Makes about 6 cones

TO MAKE THE CONES

TAKE A SHEET OF A4 PAPER AND CUT IN HALF GIVING YOU TWO A5 SHEETS. HOLDING THE PAPER LANDSCAPE-WISE, TAKE THE TOP RIGHT CORNER AND BRING IT DOWN TO MEET THE BOTTOM LEFT.

YOU WILL FORM A CONE SHAPE, WHICH CAN BE JUST TURNED UP AT THE BOTTOM AND SECURED WITH A STAPLE.

MAKE THE INSERTS WITH KITCHEN PARCHMENT PAPER IN THE SAME WAY, BUT JUST TWIST THE BOTTOM INSTEAD OF STAPLING.

Method
Slice the fish fillet, at an angle, into strips about 3/4 cm wide. You should get between 6 and 8 strips per fillet, depending on size. Toss these goujons in the seasoned flour, pat off any excess, and then coat in the beaten egg wash. Drain off any excess and then coat the fish in the breadcrumbs. Roll the goujons, gently, between your two palms to form even, rounded-edged strips. You can now cover and refrigerate until required.

For service, ideally, you should use a thermostat-controlled deep fat fryer between 175° and 195°C. Failing this, heat a pan of oil to this temperature. This can be dangerous and you should keep a constant eye on it. Make the sure the oil doesn't come more than 3/4 of the way up to the pan. It is up to temperature when a cube of fresh bread browns in 1 minute. Fry the chips, season with salt and keep warm in the oven while you deep-fry the goujons. Put a few chips in the bottom of each cone and then add two or three goujons.

Serve with little bowls of tartare sauce and a bottle of malt vinegar.

To make the tartare sauce, just add the chopped capers and parsley to the mayonnaise and stir well.

Chocolate Brownie with cherry beer sauce

I've come across a lot of chocolate brownie recipes in my time, and no two are quite the same. I think this is by far the best – thank you Jason, ex- head chef of Lettuce party design. It's rich, moist and quite simply irresistible (unlike Jason!) I've added the cherry beer sauce simply because the Lambic fruit beers of Belgium really come into their own when combined with chocolate – both as cooking ingredient and accompaniment.

Ingredients

For the cherry beer sauce
200g fresh, pitted cherries,
200ml Kriek cherry beer
1 tbsp caster sugar

For the brownie
350g hot melted butter
530g sugar
45g cocoa powder
150g plain flour
half a pint of beaten egg
a few drops of vanilla essence
200g chopped walnuts
300g plain chocolate (min 70% cocoa solids – broken into pieces)

Method
To make the sauce, bring the beer to the boil and skim off any froth. Add the cherries, bring back to the boil and simmer for five minutes. Strain off the beer, set aside the cherries and return the beer to the pan. Add the sugar and reduce to a syrup (there should be about 1 tablespoon of liquid left when its ready). Put the cherries back in the syrup and blitz with a hand blender. If you want an extra smooth sauce, pass the blitzed mixture through a fine sieve. Leave to cool, then refrigerate until required.

To make the brownie, pre-heat the oven to 180°C. Lightly butter an ovenproof dish (approx. 28cm x 17cm x 5cm deep). Combine all the ingredients in a large mixing bowl and work together until fully combined. Pour the mixture into the dish and bake in the oven for 45-50 minutes. Allow to fully cool before attempting to cut. To serve, cut into bite-size squares and drizzle over the cherry sauce – or serve in a bowl as a dip.

Here's one I burnt earlier...

Index

Recipes are shown in orange
References to items and ingredients are in **black**

Fine beer stockists

All the major supermarkets, Oddbins and Selfridges now stock an excellent range of regional and speciality beers and below I have listed some excellent specialist outlets.

Beer Ritz
17 Market Place
Knaresborough
Harrogate
North Yorkshire
HG5 8AL
Tel: 01423 862850
www.beerritz.co.uk

Beer Ritz
14 Weetwood Lane
Far Headingly
Leeds
Yorkshire
LS16 5LX
Tel: 01132 753464
www.beerritz.co.uk

Jug and Bottle
Main Street
Bubwith
East Riding of Yorkshire
Y08 6LT
Tel: 01757 289707
www.jugandbottle.co.uk

The Archer Road Beer Stop
57 Archer Road
Sheffield
Yorkshire
S8 0JT
Tel: 0114 255 1356

Barrels and Bottles
3 Oak Street
Heeley Bridge
Yorkshire
S8 9UB
Tel: 0114 255 6611
www.barrelsandbottles.co.uk

The Real Ale Shop
47 Lovat Road
Preston
Lancashire
PR1 6DQ
Tel: 01772 201591

Beers of Europe
Garage Lane
Setchey
Kings Lynn
Norfolk
PE33 0DE
Tel: 01553 812000
www.realbeerbox.com

The Alestore
70 Mytchett Road
Camberley
Surrey
GU16 6EZ
Tel: 01252 511935
www.alestore.co.uk

The Beer Shop
14 Pitfield Street
London
N1 6EY
Tel: 0207 739 3701
www.pitfieldbeershop.co.uk

Utobeer
@ Borough Market
Southwark Street
London
SE1 1TL
Tel: 020 7394 8601
www.utobeer.co.uk

Peckham and Rye
21 Clarence Drive
Glasgow
Scotland
G12 9QN
Tel: 0141 334 4312
www.peckhams.com

Peckham and Rye
155 – 159 Bruntsfield Place
Edinburgh
Scotland
EH10 3DG
Tel: 0131 229 7054
www.peckhams.com